David and Winifred -

With love, and much
admiration for all that you
achieve in our Parish -

Andrew

12·xi·05

A DIPLOMAT
AND HIS BIRDS

A DIPLOMAT
AND HIS BIRDS

Andrew Palmer

Tiercel
PUBLISHING

ISBN 0 9532002 4 8

First published 2005

Tiercel PUBLISHING 2 Mill Walk Wheathampstead Herts AL4 8DT

A catalogue record for this book is available.

For Davina, with love.

CONTENTS

PHOTOGRAPHS

House of Lords

The Right Hon. the Lord Carrington, KG.

FOREWORD

Andrew Palmer has been a friend of mine for many years. He was an accomplished diplomat, an organiser of an international conference of which I was Chairman and on whose skill I wholly relied, a zealous and energetic member of the Council of the University of Reading and much more besides. I did not, however, know that he was both a talented photographer and a lover of birds.

The photographs in this book have been a revelation to me of his skill and patience; they are accompanied by an account of how they came about and some of the amusing circumstances in which they were taken – not least his Cuban experiences. He keeps reminding his readers of his status as a total amateur. His readers will discount this and thoroughly enjoy his enthusiasm and his lively approach to the writing of this book.

Carrington

In Britain alone a million or more people profess an interest in birds. Worldwide, ornithology, birdwatching, 'birding' and 'twitching' (not to mention pigeon racing, cagebird keeping, falconry, egg collecting, wildfowling and other such pursuits) have huge followings that reflect humanity's attraction to this arm (or wing?) of the natural world. That does not mean that we all necessarily *admire* birds; interest in them can be commercial or scientific or sporting, and the 'twitching' end of the birdy spectrum has become a markedly competitive hobby with the birds themselves reduced to names in tick lists. How refreshing, therefore, is Andrew Palmer's approach: his admiration and love of birds shine from every page.

Bee-eaters and kingfishers and their kind have filled my working life. Some years ago Andrew contacted me about the albino European or golden Bee-eater that he discovered in Rome, and we have corresponded on avian matters ever since. It soon became apparent that he is a man of many parts, not only career diplomat, birdwatcher and photographer, but linguist, traveller, family man, entertaining raconteur and most able writer. In the pages of this delightful book you will find all of these attributes, and more.

Through the eye of his camera are seen not only the aesthetic qualities of bird portraiture, feathers and flight, but also revelations about biology. Here are evocative images of that lovely bird the Little Egret, its elegance and vitality captured with the counterpoint of still water and flowing plumes – photographic music, pure artistry. And the unexpected facts? Well, pictures of woodpeckers as lizard- and berry-eaters had me reaching for the textbooks. It turns out that such observations have been made before, but how inspiring to see them demonstrated photographically.

It reminds me that it was the camera (rather than binoculars) that first demonstrated that, on rare occasions, bee-eaters catch fish and kingfishers catch bees. It all goes to show that such dedicated amateurs as the author of *A Diplomat and his Birds* can still contribute meaningfully, in this age of professionalism, to science, as well as, self-evidently, to art and literature.

Professor C Hilary Fry MA PhD DSc

The immediate genesis of this little book came from the encouragement of some close friends, notably my brother-in-law David Keown-Boyd. My wife Davina and I are in the habit – following my late father's tradition – of using a photograph of a bird, which I have taken during the year, as our Christmas card. For a while now David has been generously insistent that it would be worth publishing a collection of these photographs; others have made the same flattering suggestion. Not without embarrassment, I eventually agreed to do my best.

Credit for the photographs that have appealed to David Keown-Boyd and others is largely due to the wizards who have brought out the best in them. For many years, Dave Swan achieved wonders with them at Hamilton's in High Wycombe: nothing was ever too much trouble for him, and he showed psychic powers in deciphering my requests, especially when these came from Rome and other faraway places. Latterly, I have had the benefit of further top quality work from Jason Maisey, who worked for a while with Dave Swan before setting up his own firm, Colour Shack, now of Beaconsfield. Simon Goodchild and his colleagues at the Image Maker in Amersham have also been invaluable.

I emphasise my immense gratitude to Colin and Val Shawyer at Tiercel Publishing. From our very first meeting, they have understood, humoured and enlightened me – and gently pointed me in the right directions. It was James Daunt of Daunt Books who initially recommended Tiercel to me: my warmest thanks to him for this and other good advice.

The generosity of Peter Carrington and Hilary Fry is evident in the two preceding pages, and that of Nicko Henderson at the end of the final chapter: I am more grateful to them than words can say. Many thanks also go to Heather Yasamee and Hermione Marshall at the FCO.

I prevailed upon several of my nearest and dearest to study the manuscript at various stages, and to comment on it. I am hugely indebted to Jamie Gladstone; Mark Swallow; Davina; my sons Rodney and Michael; my daughter-in-law Vanessa; my sister-in-law JoJo; and everyone else whose arm I twisted and who responded with patient and instructive suggestions.

If I were to name absolutely everyone else who has helped me in one way or another, the list would become unmanageable. As the visible tip of the iceberg, let me mention all the team at Amersham Business Services, and David Simmonds; and I cannot omit Basil, whose gimlet eye has watched over me from the first word that I typed, right through to the last.

1. Symmetry: Greater Flamingo (Phoenicopterus ruber)*, near Gacholle Lighthouse, Camargue, France, 1997*

BIRDS: WHY?

The French plumber looked with amused interest at my photograph of a group of penguins, on a bookcase in our little house in the Var.

"Where did you see those birds?" he asked.

"The Falkland Islands," I replied. "You know – *les Iles Malouines*."

"Aha – so you went to war for these!"

I said that, while this would be going too far, I knew of no diplomatic colleague who attached more importance to birds than I did – and surely many French people, as well as Britons, enjoyed watching them.

That conversation took place in 1983. My enthusiasm for observing birds, and the urge to record them in photographs, have since grown steadily. They are not alone: I have found life to be full of fascinating ingredients, each with the capacity to make me feel lucky to be enjoying them, and with a hunger for more. If I try to list them, they spin through my mind in threes. Love, family and friendship are constants. Other examples are:–

Laughter, wit, deflation of the smug (impossible, all too often);

History, Politics, Romance Languages;

Michelangelo, El Greco, Cézanne;

Mozart, Beethoven, Puccini;

Bob Dylan, Leonard Cohen, Norah Jones;

Hamlet, Great Expectations, War and Peace;

Evelyn Waugh, Anthony Powell, David Lodge;

John Le Carré, Frederick Forsyth, Gerald Seymour;

Cricket, Football, Baseball;

Hampshire CCC, Burnley FC, the Boston Red Sox;

Don Bradman (I saw him play at Lord's in 1948), Gary Sobers, Ian Botham;

Stanley Matthews, Pele, Thierry Henry;

Oysters, Fillet Steak, Raspberries;

Vodka, Chablis, Claret;

Tom Stoppard, Michael Frayn, Woody Allen;

Spike Milligan, Peter Cook, Ronnie Barker;

Fawlty Towers, Yes Minister, Dad's Army;

Dogs, fishing, gardening;

Roses, Bougainvillea, Hibiscus.

The list is more than a self-indulgent babble from Pseuds' Corner: it seeks to demonstrate that the competition from a wide range of alternative attractions has always been strong. But, whereas the others have ebbed and flowed over time, the twin passions that inspire this book consistently exert a growing and singular force on me.

I find birds increasingly life-enhancing. It is easy to take them for granted in our parallel occupation of Earth's surface (with *Homo sapiens* the newcomer by many millions of years). But for me their mastery of air, water and gravity is miraculous: we coexist with them, yet they spend much of their time in elements that we can only attain artificially; and they are so beautiful.

I started to take photographs of birds to help me to establish their identities. I then found that, when I see the gleam of a bird's eye through binoculars, or succeed in capturing its image through a telephoto lens, I feel that I am achieving some access – however superficial – to their universe. A photograph preserves such moments and, however imperfect the result, it does not harm the bird – in contrast to the regular practice among enthusiasts of former times, who shot and stuffed their targets, while my own generation used in their youth to raid birds' nests for the egg collections that were so long in vogue.

As one seeks some deeper understanding of birds, anthropomorphism is inevitable, and with it the risk of sentimentality. I try to control this tendency and to remember that the behaviour of birds is governed primarily by instinct; but I cannot escape it altogether. Moreover, humans do have characteristics in common with birds. Colour and sound play a major part in the lives of both. There are also some parallels in marital arrangements: several common bird species are largely monogamous for life, including Mute Swan, Grey Partridge, Red Grouse, Lapwing, Curlew and Oystercatcher, along with most owls and birds of prey. It must be admitted, on the other hand, that the bigamous and even polygamous habits of certain others, notably the Dunnock and the Wren, would if replicated in humans provide lurid headlines for the tabloid press. There are meanwhile some amusing comparisons in our respective handling of parental responsibilities, of which more later.

There is also fascination in the huge variety of bird species: globally, there are as many as 10,000, and each has developed its own particular system for living, feeding and reproducing. There is, moreover, virtually no interbreeding between species: one does not find hybrid or mongrel birds, except among ducks.

Overall, however, such attempts as I have made at a more rigorously scientific approach have tended to founder on my preference for a good photograph. I am thus a self-indulgent opportunist, and sometimes a shameless dilettante, in my admiration of birds. It would anyway be pretentious for me to claim any profound value for my subjective and fleeting ornithological insights. More than anything, the driving forces are simple curiosity, wonderment and – why not admit it? – pleasure. Some of the aesthetic grounds for this will, I hope, speak for themselves through the photographs. Enchantment by birds must also, like it or not, have some psychological dimension: though I should prefer to spare the reader, and myself, any very intimate discussion of this, I happily declare my belief that birdwatching and bird photography have real therapeutic value.

I first experienced a comparable benefit through trout fishing. When I was a desk officer in busy departments in the Foreign and Common-wealth Office (FCO) in London, I would return to Buckinghamshire after a hectic week, with unresolved issues nagging at my mind and conscience. Therapy was close at hand. Since 1968, I have been a member of the syndicate fishing the lake, and a mile of the River Wye, at West Wycombe Park, now the home of Edward and Lucinda Dashwood. The latest screen version of *The Importance of Being Earnest* confirms that this is an idyllic place. Amid the temples, follies and immaculately landscaped grounds, the water is very clear. Especially on the river, stealth and light tackle are essential. The strategy and tactics are wholly absorbing, whether approaching a pool; establishing that some fish are rising; deciding how best to simulate the fly on which they are feeding; or finally attempting to present it without alarming them. Concentration must remain total. Hours pass in a flash. One returns tired but contented. I found consistently that, when Monday dawned, so did solutions to difficulties that had seemed intractable the previous Friday or Saturday.

The absorption of finding, observing and photographing birds entails similar phases to fishing, and has brought me still greater advantages which have of course been far more readily accessible, even when life has been dominated by serious pressures. This process has applied to others, at the very highest levels. The War Diaries of Field Marshal Lord Alanbrooke show how the Chief of the Imperial General Staff in World War II was invigorated by a carefully planned excursion to photograph sea birds in 1943. In July 1945, when the war was nearly over but his responsibilities still most demanding, Alanbrooke took a short time off to photograph a Hobby, that attractive migratory falcon. Amid the entries about strategy and politics, the imminent defeat of Japan and his relationship with Winston Churchill, the Field Marshal recorded that he had left his precious films to be developed, praying that they would be good. How well I know that feeling.

Once under their spell, birds have provided a particularly rewarding learning curve for me. When one first discovers a feature of their behaviour, it can appear striking, endearing or even comical; but it always proves to have a good reason behind it. For example, my wife Davina and I thought we were seeing things when, near Rome, we observed more than two adult Bee-eaters bringing food to a single nest – but then we read that it was quite usual for birds who had not paired off to act as 'helpers' in this admirably collective way. My dear friend (and Davina's first cousin) Jamie Gladstone and I found it bizarre that some Shelduck by the Solway Firth appeared to be nesting in rabbit burrows – but the books assured us that it was normal for them to make the most of such ready-made homes. Once such details have been noticed, there is every chance of their recurring in subsequent sightings of the species in question, wherever these may occur.

I am not a sufficiently expert photographer, let alone ornithologist, to warrant my writing a straightforward presentation of a few dozen photographs, accompanied merely by an account of how each was taken. To compensate, I shall attempt some reflections on how I came to be seeking out birds in particular places at various times, and what were then my other priorities; and some thoughts on what some of the pictures evoke for me. In case these become tedious, I plead that my main purpose is not self-indulgent reminiscence: I seek rather to celebrate the beauty of birds and my good fortune in having witnessed it quite widely.

In other words, I want – in that rather ghastly phrase – to share these joys with others.

This account will begin in Cuba in the mid-1980s: that was where I first took photography at all seriously. But, alongside many other excitements, the magic of birds had gradually been taking hold in most of our previous overseas postings.

In all, I was exceptionally fortunate in the jobs that came my way thanks to the FCO, at home as well as abroad, and in the qualities of the great majority of the colleagues and contacts with whom I worked. The career was every bit as rewarding as I had anticipated in the beginning – though it was also a good deal more strenuous.

My first overseas assignment was to run the commercial section in the Embassy in La Paz from 1963 to 1965. Bolivia is a huge and spectacular country, with friendly people. Its mineral resources have been central to much of its history. Its leaders have not found it easy to remain in power: since Bolivia gained independence in 1825, there have been some 190 *coups d'état* there. We witnessed the overthrow of the centre-left government of President Victor Paz Estenssoro in 1964, after his party had been in power for twelve years (and he would return later). We felt personally affected, having got to know the President's charming son Ramiro Paz while he was at the London School of Economics earlier in the 1960s; he had returned to run a department for economic development in his father's government. The President and all his family got away to the airport and safety; our English nanny, having befriended her counterpart who looked after the younger Paz children, had learned that their bags had been packed for some days before the coup.

Bolivia's geography provides dramatic juxtapositions: orange trees against a background of snow-capped peaks, for example. Views in the capital are dominated by the 22,000-foot mountain Illimani. The foreground in our garden included flower-beds where hummingbirds fed; tanagers were also regular visitors. This was my introduction to watching exotic birds. The greatest thrills came, however, when we were fishing or sight-seeing up in the mountains and saw mighty Andean Condors, the awesome emblem of those regions, soaring above the peaks and glaciers with their wingspan of ten feet.

We moved on to Ottawa, where from 1965 to 1967 I was the low man on the totem pole of the political section of the High Commission. The lead-in to Canada's centennial year in 1967 generated much intriguing analysis of the nation's role. The emphasis became less introspective with the magnificent festivities of Expo 67 in Montreal, attended by many overseas leaders. But then President de Gaulle arrived and made his infamous declaration of *"Vive le Québec libre!"* which recklessly inflamed separatist feelings. The charismatic Pierre Trudeau, himself a *Québecois*, was then rising to dominance in the Canadian political scene; it would take all his courage and ingenuity to devise a constructive way ahead amid these passions.

There is wonderful countryside around Ottawa. My most memorable birdwatching moments occurred when fishing on lakes to the north, when I regularly saw Great Northern Divers – fabulous birds, known there by the less stirring name of Loons.

France has become so integral to our life – and to my birdwatching – that I deal with it separately. Readers who persevere as far as Chapter 11 will find that, amid some thoughts on the Camargue, it looks back at some of the thrills and spills of working with the media in Paris from 1972 until 1976. In many ways this was the most intensively active of all my overseas experiences. Such at any rate was the perception of my susceptible ego at the time; and birdwatching and other reflective pursuits were temporarily marginalised.

Our next spell abroad was in Oslo, from 1979 to 1982, as head of the political section and for the last year or so deputy head of mission, under the stimulating leadership of Archie Lamb and, latterly, Gill Brown. We maintained a very close dialogue with the Norwegians over the security of the northern flank of the North Atlantic Treaty Organisation (NATO), where Norway – sharing a frontier with the Soviet Union – was strategically located. Politico-military issues generated by the Cold War were always gripping. In 1981, the State Visit by HM The Queen was a major highlight of our time in Oslo.

The Norwegians were great people to work with: expert, frank and supremely accessible. One morning shortly after our arrival, there had been disturbing news of the movements of Soviet submarines. I sought a meeting with the senior Norwegian official principally concerned, Leif

Mevik, of whom I had heard many good things but had not then met. He rang back in a few moments.

"Mr Palmer? I should be delighted to see you, but I'm afraid that I must ask you to wait . . ." – my heart began to sink – ". . . wait until 11.30."

Leif was in effect apologising for seeing me that very same morning. This level of generosity was maintained by many other excellent Norwegian friends, not least Magne Hagen, Private Secretary to His Majesty King Olav, throughout the months of preparation for the State Visit: it was as great a pleasure to deal with Magne as it was with the impeccable Robert Fellowes at Buckingham Palace.

Our garden in Oslo was home to families of Green and Great Spotted Woodpeckers, Nuthatches and other birds. It was there that my family became aware that I was getting more and more out of observing these lovely creatures, and the seabirds in Oslo Fjord. I was still wholly clueless at that point – for some time I thought that the maniacal laugh of the Green Woodpecker must come from some over-excited seagull.

The real addiction was still to come.

2. Early morning flight: West Indian Woodpecker (Melanerpes superciliaris), *Jibacoa, Cuba, 1987*

*I*t is shortly before dawn on the north coast of Cuba. A solitary figure, laden with photographic equipment, picks his way along the wooded creek by the estuary of the Jibacoa River. There is no sound, even from the wavelets of the Strait of Florida that lap the empty beach behind him. The chill, the half-light and the man's shortage of sleep should, according to the military adage that he recalls, reduce his alertness and lower his spirits. But his laboured progress belies his determination, which will shortly give way to high excitement. He knows that, as the sun comes up to warm the creek and its surrounding vegetation, its denizens will come to life, always in the same order, each operating in its specific environmental niche. They will emerge tentatively at first, then work busily, with mounting sound and vigour, until they retire in the mid-day heat.

He comes level with two dead trees, barely thirty feet apart, and twice that distance from his track. One is a palm; the other, dead for much longer, nondescript. He retreats to the east of the two trees, into the rudimentary cover that he has been working sporadically to improve. He grapples with his tripod, checks his lenses and spare films. A round hole drilled in the palm tree, some fifteen feet above the ground, is already becoming discernible. He brings its image into his viewfinder and fixes it there with levers on the tripod. Before the morning is out, a family group of birds with which he has become agreeably familiar, West Indian Woodpeckers, will have appeared there. The rarer, endemic Cuban Green Woodpecker is nesting in the other tree: the fledglings are due to emerge. He gives his binoculars a final wipe. Everything is ready.

*   *   *

The above passage is taken from the uncompleted manuscript of a novel that I have attempted to write (in it, the birdwatcher's attention is soon distracted by occurrences with melodramatic political significance). Perhaps this other *oeuvre* may one day find its way into print from its present resting place in my "pending/too difficult" tray. I am giving the paragraphs an airing here in the hope that they convey, as accurately as I can achieve it, my feelings on those enchanted dawn outings as I studied those woodpeckers *(Photographs 2 and 3)*.

3. Not our first choice, but . . . Cuban Green Woodpecker (Xiphidiopicus percussus), *Jibacoa, 1987*

In finding myself in that spot, and for that matter in more manicured parts of Cuba, I frequently found it difficult to believe my good fortune. We were posted to run the British Embassy in Havana in the summer of 1986, remaining there until late in 1988. It was a job that we had always wanted, ever since I was assigned in 1961 to the Department in the Foreign Office dealing with Latin America. We were not disappointed; and we could not have been there at a more absorbing time.

The personality of Fidel Castro still dominated all aspects of life in Cuba; the apparent enigma of his relationship with the Cuban people continued to fascinate me. The *Comandante's* durability seemed remarkable enough even then, 19 years before the time of writing; I regard it as phenomenal now.

As ever, the foreign policy dimensions were most intriguing. A joke that did the rounds in Havana during our time there put the question "what is the largest nation in the world?" The answer – "Cuba, which has its government in Moscow, its army in Africa, and its people in Florida" – was a fair indication of the range of international equations that were complicated by Cuban factors. From a population of little over ten million, the overseas projection of Cuban armed force and medical expertise was extraordinary. But it was not disproportionate to Fidel's ambitions: he made it clear that, having achieved leadership of the Cuban nation and made it truly 'independent' at last, he sought Cuban leadership of Latin America and of the Non-Aligned Movement.

Of the superpowers, the Reagan Administration in Washington saw Castro and his regime as not merely an outpost of the Evil Empire less than 100 miles from their shores: it was a significant military ally of the main adversary of the USA. Havana's insistence that the 30,000 Cuban troops in Angola were assisting the recognised government there against guerrillas supported by South Africa cut no ice in Western capitals, least of all in the White House. There, the key factor was that in Angola and in other far-flung theatres Cuban forces were serving the interests of the Soviet Union.

Characteristically, contradictions were not far away. President Gorbachev had come to power in 1985 and, by the time we arrived in Havana, there was promising momentum in the dialogue between

Washington and Moscow. It would bear fruit at the strategic and other levels, bringing change to many areas. But psychological and domestic political considerations in the USA continued to inhibit any such *détente* with neighbouring Cuba. The United States did not – and still does not – have full diplomatic relations with Castro, and they maintained their economic blockade on Cuba. For his part, Castro continued to make the most of opportunities – spurious and otherwise – to claim that US actions vindicated his endless calls for vigilance and "combativity," and his other rhetorical attacks on US "imperialism". Thus, a sonic boom by an American jet fighter over Cuba made headlines in the Cuban media for days on end, purporting to demonstrate that the "look-out-they're-coming" element of Fidelism was correct all along.

At the same time, we became aware of the first twitching of the rug that Gorbachev was to pull from beneath Fidel. Senior Soviet diplomats in Havana had previously been full of fraternal solidarity with their hosts (when not totally tight-lipped on emerging from their ghastly phallic tower of an Embassy). But they now moved on from bland evasions to open criticism of Cuban economic mismanagement. We thus witnessed the first discernible impact on Cuba of Gorbachev's remedies of *glasnost* and *perestroika*. At the time, public allusions to them by the Cubans themselves were still rare: Castro finessed questions of "openness" and, to the extent that he was prepared to mention "restructuring" at all, he insisted that it could not be the appropriate solution for Cuba. He also predicted that Gorbachev's policies, especially *perestroika*, would be disastrous for the Soviet Union.

With this, one sensed growing alarm that the whole basis for Cuba's sugar-for-oil arrangements with the USSR could become precarious. This trade, established at the cost of deepening Cuba's reliance on the crop from which Castro's revolution had initially promised diversification, was in the mid-1980s still a reasonably healthy source of foreign exchange for him. Much of this came from Soviet (and Angolan) oil, acquired cheaply in exchange for sugar and sold on while still on the high seas. Such largesse was not on Gorbachev's agenda.

For Britain, the implications of all this were tantalising. Cuban perceptions of Britain as Reagan's best friend were accurate enough; but they could be offset by the knowledge that the UK had never been at one with Washington on the possible merit of the US embargo on Cuba. Our exports to Cuba in 1986 stood at £60m – our fifth largest market in Latin America, with machinery and chemicals for the sugar industry the main items. Against this background, we hoped that we were well placed to give frank explanations of Western policies; and British and Cuban Ministers had agreed to work realistically for a step-by-step improvement in our bilateral relations.

Constructive engagement was also the approach preferred by our partners in the (then) European Community. But, while trade and investment were not so formally conditional on human rights improvements as they were to become in the Common Position of the European Union ten years later, the EC resolved to bring concerted pressure to bear along these lines. As the UK held the Presidency of the EC during my first six months in Havana, we were in the front line; and representations on human rights were not a short cut to popularity there.

Our work thus entailed challenges. It could bring rewards. We tried, without compromising our stand on human rights, to make the most of uncontroversial commercial and cultural projects. Visits by several major UK Chambers of Commerce opened important doors in Havana. Major financial and industrial players from Britain showed interest in joint ventures with Cuban State enterprises. Alongside the likes of Canada, Mexico and Spain, we still seemed in quite a good position to assist the overdue diversification of the Cuban economy.

Throughout, as was perhaps inevitable in a land where paradox and illusion are plentiful, both elation and despair could come from unexpected directions. At a moment when Cuban resentment of the Western Europeans' stance on Castro's human rights record was acute, I received the rare privilege of a summons from Fidel, across the room at one of his receptions for a visiting dignitary. The President warmly charged me to report a significant new flexibility in his views on the possibility of the withdrawal of Cuban forces from Angola.

Either way, the spontaneous charm and laughter of the Cuban people were never far away, and the large island – it is longer than Great Britain – provides innumerable scenic, cultural and historical treats. These have, since our time in Cuba, become more accessible to European tourists: when we were there, Castro did not greatly encourage the development of tourism, while he could still earn foreign currency through the sugar-for-oil barter that was so much more palatable to him ideologically.

My enjoyment of the company of Cubans and of their culture, in the broadest sense, also produced some clues as to why, for many of them, Fidel Castro has not been the ogre depicted in some Western circles. Yes, his rule has been tyrannical. Yes, he only broke away from domination by the neighbouring superpower through dependence on another, whose demise then left him isolated, though not before the Cuban variant of Marxism had stifled natural enterprise there. But, in the 1980s, there were still plenty of Cubans with lurid memories of the fiendish Batista, overthrown by Castro's revolution in 1959: they emphasised that almost anything was preferable to the return of the former dictator's murderous cronies, lurking and plotting in Miami. (The exiles and refugees in the USA also included erstwhile supporters of Castro himself, disenchanted with his Communism and his abuses of human rights). Meanwhile, Castro's regular appearances on the world stage gave pride to his people. In my time, such events as the visit of the Spanish Prime Minister Felipe González – the first serving head of government of an EC nation to visit Cuba – and the restoration of relations with most of the other Latin American countries confirmed that Fidel had not run out of panache or influence

Castro was masterly in playing the Hispanic card. The Creole landowners who started Wars of Independence in the nineteenth century were presented not as the heirs of Spanish colonialist oppressors but as "freedom fighters" who had taken up arms for the liberation of slaves. The fathers of both of the formative Cuban nationalists – José Martí and Castro himself – were born in Spain, which added to the intensity of Castro's argument, quoting extensively if selectively from Martí, that Cuba was the front line in the protection of the regenerated values of *Hispanidad* against the threat from the brutal Anglo-Saxon North. This was also an instance of the ambivalence of Cuban views of the USA: many of them did not deny the successes of the capitalist system there, however alien they might regard it for Cuba.

I did not meet Castro anything like as frequently as some of my successors did, but we saw enough of the *Comandante* in person to feel the impact of his charisma, and to appreciate his phenomenal powers of recall in pursuing a conversation from the point reached at a previous meeting. For example, at another of the President's own receptions, I was showing Commonwealth solidarity in chatting with our newly-appointed colleague from Zimbabwe, who wore an elegant pin-striped suit. Fidel remarked that he had once had a similar outfit. I commented that *The Early Fidel* by Lionel Martin of the BBC included a photograph of him thus attired; and striped suits remained a light-hearted theme in my subsequent conversations with Castro, occasional though these were. This vignette made us realise what an asset the President's formidable memory must be in achieving feel-good effects with his own people, at all levels throughout Cuba.

On ceremonial occasions, the seats on the platform for the Diplomatic Corps were sometimes level with Fidel's podium, and close enough to see that he delivered his speeches of three hours and more with the aid of only a single small piece of paper. The structure, the allusions, the long lists of what, say, *el Che* would have thought and done about one set of revolutionary shortcomings, and then another, were all consistently ordered and magisterially delivered, for the most part without reference even to the few notes before him. Time spent in the presence of Fidel in full oratorical flow passed remarkably quickly, provided that you felt that you were still abreast of the scheme of what he was saying.

There was also the Yoruba dimension: the people who constituted the majority of the slaves brought from Africa to Cuba (and to Brazil, where racial harmony has also generally prevailed). Successive colleagues from this people's native land of Nigeria – one a Yoruba, the other not – emphasised to me their conviction that the Yorubas' happy disposition was a key factor in the political acquiescence as well as the personal charm of most Afro-Cubans. Yorubas are artistically gifted, notably in the rhythms of their music and the allure of their painting, much of it replete with the symbolism of *santería,* the syncretist cult created by Yoruba slaves who disguised their native deities by giving them the identities of Christian Saints. All this provided Cubans of Yoruba descent, and many others related or connected to them, with outlets that did not seriously threaten Fidel's control, while contributing massively to the overall vitality of Cuban culture, already rich in its Hispanic heritage.

The international standing of contemporary Cuban music (the Buena Vista Social Club, Arturo Sandoval), ballet (Alicia Alonso, Carlos Acosta) and painting (Wifredo Lam, Rene Portocarrero) is eloquent testimony to the success of this happy blend.

Another rich seam of Cuban talent emerged in sporting arenas. In our time in Havana, Castro withdrew from the 1988 Olympic Games in Seoul out of "fraternal solidarity" with North Korea. But over the years a disproportionate number of famous world and Olympic champions and record holders, such as the athletes Alberto Juantorena, Javier Sotomayor and Ana Fidelia Quirot, and the boxer Teofilo Stevenson, have come from Cuba's relatively small population. They have also frequently won international baseball tournaments; having become hooked on the game in Boston, I regularly enjoyed watching encounters at the *Estadio Latinoamericano*.

*   *   *

Our house in Havana, once the home of a 'Sugar Baron' was suitably exotic. It had an ornate indoor swimming pool – covered, we were told, because the original owner did not wish female members of his family to be visible to outsiders when swimming. The airy house and its spacious garden, full of Italianate adornments, were ideal for both our official and our family purposes.

There were plenty of birds around our home, too, especially when a range of colourful warblers migrating between North and South America visited our garden. Our resident species meanwhile provided regular entertainment, prompting comparison with spectacular bird behaviour that we had witnessed elsewhere. A Cuban Emerald – a hummingbird – habitually attacked itself in the mirror on our covered terrace, in the manner of the male Northern Cardinals that we had seen in Boston, furiously flying at their own scarlet images in the hub-caps and wing mirrors of parked cars.

The Mockingbirds in our garden suffered from no such problems regarding their own identity and those of potential adversaries: they swooped fearlessly to harass anything or anyone – cats, dogs, humans – that they deemed a threat to their nest or their young. One of them frequently used the flagpole as his lookout point and launching pad, thus adding further panache both to the Union Jack and to his own exploits *(4 and 5)*. These assaults prompted respectful comparison with the even more violent attacks of the Arctic Terns that we had seen in Spitzbergen, during our time in Norway. Notwithstanding their elegant and super-ficially benign appearance, those birds were in such deadly earnest in the defence of their nests that Nordic locals passing innocently nearby carried stout sticks to protect themselves from the threat of a severe pecking. (The Arctic Tern is even more remarkable for its migration between the Arctic and Antarctic regions: it is determined to spend as much time as it possibly can in daylight, and for this purpose it commutes some 10,000 miles twice a year, from pole to pole).

Meanwhile, we revelled in our sub-tropical surroundings. Our street ran downhill to the Malecón, the broad promenade that sweeps along five miles of Havana's faded but graceful seafront. From our upper windows we could see the occasional Magnificent Frigate Bird – so well named – soaring above the glistening sea; Brown Pelicans and other sea birds flew past.

But it was at Jibacoa that we found our principal bird-watching riches. In this small seaside village some 40 miles east of the capital, the Embassy owned a house on a promontory between two idyllic beaches, with a coral reef and brilliantly coloured fish in easy reach, and safe swimming for families. Its previous owner fled to Florida shortly after Castro's Revolution in 1959; as he left, he reportedly tossed the keys to a member of the staff of the British Embassy, asking that the house be well cared for. All our home-based colleagues were encouraged to make full use of this heavenly facility at weekends; and one could reserve a room for Friday and Saturday nights.

For me this accommodation was by night 'sleeping' in name only: the heat, and the salsa music rending the air from a neighbouring establish-ment, remained all-pervasive until the early hours. When, finally, the temperature became comfortably cool, and the revellers departed, deep sleep did become possible – but, once I had become enthralled by the birds, my repose lasted only until my alarm sounded under my pillow and I set off for the creek before first light. I did my re-charging in the afternoons, when a long swim and a large *mojito* – a delicious but

4. *Action stations in our Havana garden: Paseo 352, Vedado, Havana, 1986*
5. *(Inset) Ready to pounce: Northern Mockingbird* (Mimus polyglottos), *Havana, 1986*

deceptive cocktail of rum and fresh lime juice – would combine to make me dead to the world.

I first became aware of the bird life at Jibacoa from the terrace of that blessed Embassy beach house. The Stripe-headed Tanager was a popular visitor *(6)*. Flocks of Cattle Egrets would leave their breeding ground in a nearby mangrove swamp to spend the day foraging on farmland; they returned, in orderly formations, in the evening. Ospreys breed in Cuba, and we were thrilled to see the occasional one hovering over the sea. My first sighting of a Belted Kingfisher, twice the length and several times the weight of the Eurasian species – though less colourful – was also offshore.

Campo, the factotum at Jibacoa, a wonderfully humorous black Cuban (his grandparents, whom he remembered, had started life as slaves), told me where I could see these kingfishers more regularly around the creek.

Campo assured me that I would also enjoy an encounter with the *Arriero,* the local name for the Great Lizard Cuckoo. He then emitted a series of ascending cackles – a sound so wicked that all Britons within range took acute alarm. But a passing trio of Cuban schoolchildren evidently recognised the bloodcurdling tones as a decent imitation of the *Arriero.* They joined in with Campo, producing a horrendous cacophony, and pointing in the direction of the creek before we all collapsed in helpless mirth.

When he had recovered, Campo solemnly told me that it was easier to hear the *Arriero* than to see it.

"No surprise there then," I ventured, "unless we have just frightened them all away."

"But no, *Señor Embajador,*" he chortled, "my calls will have brought more *Arrieros* in to Jibacoa. And it will be possible for you to see one – but only if you get up early in the morning."

I realised that I could not side-step this challenge. Thus began the habit that was to bring me so much interest and happiness for the rest of our time in Cuba.

The following morning, I indecisively surveyed the creek. The dawn light was becoming brighter, and various birds were moving. Among the earliest to appear in the surrounding palm trees was a group of Cuban Blackbirds. Endemic to Cuba, this cheerful bird, known as the *'Toti'* after

6. *Welcome visitor: Stripe-headed Tanager* (Spindalis zena), *Jibacoa, 1986*

7. *Bright eye, raucous voice: Great Lizard Cuckoo* (Saurothera merlini), *Jibacoa, 1986*

its call, is ubiquitous there. In the water, the first to show was a Green Heron, poised motionless on a sunken log as it awaited its prey. Looking further along the creek, I could identify the undulating flight of some woodpeckers. One pair looked larger than the others, but both types seemed to have business in the same area of the creek. A dead palm tree helped me to mark down their destination for investigation later.

This planning was interrupted by a disturbance in some bushes a short distance away. Some creature was moving from branch to branch, approaching my position. I froze. The clumsy progress continued. This was surely no bird – what exotic animal would it prove to be? Closer and closer it came, with occasional pauses and sounds of scrabbling. The bush beside me was identical, but I did not dare to believe that the creature could be about to appear above my head. It did arrive, though, in a series of flops and lurches. It was a bird after all – almost two feet long, chestnut and white in colour, with bright orange eyes and a long, wide, striped tail. It settled some ten feet above my head. I was almost literally face to face with a Great Lizard Cuckoo. I had seen from the books that it is bigger by one third than its European cousin; at this range it seemed larger still.

The main lens for my Leica at the time was an 80-200 millimetre zoom – wonderfully reliable, but not exactly long-range. However, with anything more powerful, it would have been very difficult to focus on this bird. Holding my breath, I took a few shots of him *(7)*. He seemed unperturbed for the moment; but his choice of perch in the sharp contrasts of the morning light was such that I needed to move if I was to get a picture with the sun more fully on him. I took the gamble. The *Arriero* did not appreciate it; as the bird departed, the strident cackle of its disapproval was familiar from Campo's performance the previous afternoon.

This encounter with a Great Lizard Cuckoo was the first of many, but none of the others was as close. I felt addicted already to watching birds around that creek; and I could not wait to tell Campo that not only had I seen the *Arriero* – I had done so before hearing its voice.

There was another feeling of contentment, less easy to define at first. It was only during the week that followed that I realised how greatly the episodes with Campo and the *Arriero* had refreshed all parts of me.

8. *Highly special: Cuban Green Woodpecker* (Xiphidiopicus percussus), *Jibacoa, 1987*

3

THE RED AND THE GREEN: WOODPECKER WEEKENDS

The combination of Fidelism, photography and family could lead in unexpected directions. The telephone in our bedroom rang, striking an under-powered, hesitant note.

"George – is that you?"

"Colonel! Great to hear you."

So began many a telephone conversation with my father. He and his elder brother, my splendid Uncle Gerald, to whom I was also close, had called me George for as long as anyone could recall. To everyone else, I was Andrew: there is no 'G' in my initials, any more than there was a 'W' in those of my father or my uncle – and they called each other Bill throughout their lives. It was just one of those things that are never explained – or two of them, to be more precise, and there was even a third. Only a matter of hours after I had arrived at Hopper's, my House at Winchester, my school-mates in what is now called one's 'peer group' began for no apparent reason to call me George. None of them had met me before, let alone heard me addressed by my father and uncle. The name remained with me throughout my five happy years at Winchester and, when I moved up the hill to the nearby Green Jackets Depot to report for my National Service, my Wykehamist friend Barry Reed naturally greeted me as George. Our cockney colleagues in that Training Company knew me as nothing else, giving the name a healthy twang. The Sergeants in charge of us did, I admit, often address me in harsher terms, which I generally deserved.

My dear father showed heroic perseverance in his early telephone calls to me in Cuba from rural Berkshire where, in 1986, it was still necessary to summon the assistance of an operator to make such a connection. The Colonel often waited hours for contact to be established. Once this had been achieved I regularly sought, as ever, his expert guidance in matters ornithological and photographic. After I had been in Havana for a couple of months, a principal topic of our conversations was the need for me to acquire a more powerful telephoto lens. As we pursued the merits of the various brands, we noticed that the delays in establishing contact between the Colonel and George were mercifully becoming shorter. Less helpful was the series of clunks and other sinister sounds that came to punctuate our exchanges – the hallmarks of what the French so deftly term a *table d'écoute*.

This seemed an acceptable price for getting through rapidly. One could not really blame the local authorities for paying attention to earnest discussions of long-range photography between two persons of whom one was manifestly using a false name, while the other's title suggested a supervisor or controller. Aware that I was not alone in hearing the Colonel's firm advice that a 500-millimetre lens was imperative for the accomplishment of my task, I took early opportunities to show some of my bird photographs, imperfect though they were, to Cuban officials.

Rod, our elder son – and namesake of the Colonel – brought out the chosen lens when he came to Havana for the Christmas of 1986. Tony Burgess, our Head of Chancery and an accomplished photographer, gave me patient advice in its use. By the turn of the year, I felt more properly equipped to record my sightings of birds in Cuba, which had become more exciting with every dawn excursion.

When I first noticed the two pairs of woodpeckers at Jibacoa, they were competing for the same tree. Woodpeckers like trees with a very hard outer shell and soft heartwood: hence the attraction of the dead palm. The victors were the larger of the two species there, named in the 1985 edition of Professor James Bond's *Birds of the West Indies* as the Cuban Red-bellied Woodpecker, with the scientific name *Melanerpes superciliaris*. Later works gave the different name of West Indian Woodpecker to this species, but the only other territories where it is found are the Bahamas and the Cayman Islands, and it is in Cuba that it is most common. The name "Cuban Red-bellied Woodpecker" rolled agreeably off the tongue; all in all I preferred to remain loyal to the work of James Bond. I confess that I was also influenced by the popular belief that it was the name of this distinguished ornithologist that was borrowed by Ian Fleming, another resident of the West Indies, as he scanned his bookshelves in Jamaica in search of a suitable name for his hero 007.

But the science has since moved on. Experts have ruled that the name Red-bellied Woodpecker applies to the closely related *Melanerpes carolinus*, found from Florida to the Great Lakes, while my Cuban friend *Melanerpes superciliaris* is regarded as a separate full species, and named the West Indian Woodpecker.

9 & 10. Arrival and departure: West Indian Woodpeckers (Melanerpes superciliaris), *Jibacoa, 1987*

These riddles of nomenclature aside, the West Indian Woodpeckers were an ideal subject for a beginner. They are noisy, active and regular in their routines, and they excavated the nest for their 1987 brood at a conveniently visible point high up in the dead palm tree. They often called as they flew across the creek towards the nest. It was thrilling to see them approach, with their bouncing flight. When they were a short distance from the tree, I would switch my attention to the viewfinder, and witness in close-up their arrival by their hole. This was not so much a landing as a brilliantly controlled impact, with the birds' very strong feet and tail enabling them to move in the blink of an eye from horizontal flight to vertical adherence to the tree *(9 and 10)*.

They set about drilling the cavity and, later, feeding their young with an intensity that evidently left them unconcerned about their alien watcher with his metallic contraptions. In case it appears, nevertheless, that I boorishly forced my presence on these birds, I plead that I cannot have disturbed them greatly, for West Indian Woodpeckers excavated another nest in the same tree the following year. (This second hole was not, unfortunately, quite so well placed for the early morning light). I like to think that it was the same pair; they were surely close relatives, at the very least.

Over the two years, the West Indian Woodpeckers provided some spectacular sights. The male and female seemed to share equally the work of constructing the nest and feeding the brood, and it was not unusual to see both birds together. Perhaps my most dramatic photograph shows the male's delivery to the nest of a lizard *(11)*, whose shadow is poignantly vivid. The female, not to be outdone, is seen arriving with four medium-sized berries in her bill *(12)*. There was an entertaining moment when two of the juveniles of 1988 appeared at each of the two cavities *(13)*.

Fortunately, one had only to move a short distance to photograph the other species. The Cuban Green Woodpecker is endemic to that country and is the smallest of the Cuban woodpeckers. The male of the pair at Jibacoa offered plucky resistance to the West Indian Woodpeckers' claim to the palm tree – the literature confirms that the Cuban Green prefers to nest in those trunks – before giving way. The other dead tree nearby where this pair settled, albeit as second best, cannot have been too

11. Some woodpeckers occasionally eat lizards: West Indian Woodpeckers, Jibacoa, 1988

12. . . . and berries, too: West Indian Woodpecker, Jibacoa, 1987

unsatisfactory, for they too returned to the same place in 1988; and I saw no further hostilities between the two species.

The Cuban Green Woodpecker is usually described as shy. The pair at Jibacoa gave the impression of being less extrovert than their West Indian neighbours. With their smaller bills, they brought home less startling trophies. But this attractive bird *(3, 8 and 14)* seemed cheerfully indomitable in its demeanour. One of them gave a good display when Rod accompanied me one early morning, and provided him with exciting viewing through the lens that he had brought out for me. Cuban friends were pleased to learn that we had spotted, and admired, their *carpintero verde*. I have since learned that *Xiphidiopicus percussus*, to give the Cuban Green Woodpecker its scientific name, is indeed a special bird. Experts have explained that its entire genus is endemic to Cuba: there is only the single species in *Xiphidiopicus,* and no other woodpecker really like the Cuban Green Woodpecker anywhere else in the Americas. (There are several with a superficial resemblance, but they are members of different sub-families and genera to the exclusive *Xiphidiopicus).*

Both the pairs of woodpeckers at Jibacoa raised their broods successfully, and I had the good fortune to see the fledglings on early sorties. Juvenile woodpeckers are a joy – to the observer, at least. Woodpeckers are one of the families of birds whose chicks are nidicolous (nest-dwelling), as opposed to nidifugous (nest-fleeing). Examples of the latter are coot or partridge chicks, which can swim or run after a mere 24 hours, and feed for themselves (though guarded by their parents). Young woodpeckers, on the other hand, stay in the nest for three to four weeks, relying entirely on their parents for food.

When they do emerge, juveniles of the nidicolous species are already approaching the size of their parents, an impression enhanced in wood-peckers by the bulk of their downy feathers. Moreover, they are pristinely clean – whereas the adults can look exhausted by the sustained efforts of parenthood, especially in a wet spring when their own feathers are slicked down and discoloured. At occasional challenging moments when our children were teenagers, Davina and I would ruefully – but affectionately – indulge in some reverse anthropomorphism, and liken our situation to that of a pair of exhausted woodpecker parents. If only we could move about with a grace comparable to the elegant rhythms of their flight.

13. Anyone else at home? Juvenile West Indian Woodpeckers, Jibacoa, 1988

14. This tree did nicely, after all: Cuban Green Woodpecker (Xiphidiopicus percussus), *Jibacoa, 1987*

15. *National pride: Cuban Trogon* ('Tocororo') (Priotelus temnurus)*, near Playa Girón, Cuba, 1988*

4

THE BAY OF BIRDS

The national bird of Cuba is the Cuban Trogon, generally known there as the *Tocororo,* after its call. It is an inspired choice. The colours of this dove-sized bird include the red, white and blue of the Cuban flag, and its velvety green upperparts evoke the beauty of its habitat. The *Tocororo* appears regularly in such material as tourist brochures, and the urge to see one was strong. I first did so at Soroa, in the western Province of Piñar del Rio, in a lush hillside orchid garden. It was sitting near the top of a tall tree, but the view of it was enough to whet the appetite still further. Over the next year, we had only a few fleeting glimpses of them. Something serious had to be done to put this right.

The idea of an excursion in quest of the lovely bird began to take shape when friends in the Foreign Ministry in Havana advised the *Cienaga de Zapata* as the best location for seeing substantial numbers of *Tocororos.* The very name 'Zapata Swamp' conjures up fantastic images – all the more so as the area includes the Bay of Pigs, the geographical feature of Cuba that became, in April 1961, a byword in the politics of the Western Hemisphere and in relations between the superpowers.

*   *   *

When John F Kennedy succeeded Dwight Eisenhower as President of the USA in January 1961, he inherited a variety of plans to dispose of Castro. Kennedy was not at first enthusiastic about armed intervention to achieve this. He attached importance to economic reform in Latin America, and had some sympathy with Castro's initial, pre-communist measures. He had expressed a desire for better relations with the Soviet Union and did not wish to jeopardise the prospects for a summit with Khrushchev.

But the new President eventually agreed to an invasion by a force of 1,500 anti-Castro Cubans, assembled in Guatemala under CIA auspices. The Zapata area was chosen for the landings as a location remote from heavily defended centres of population: the strategy was to give the para-military troops time to establish a beachhead, from which a provisional alternative government would be established. This would provide a springboard for an anti-Castro uprising throughout Cuba – and a pretext for a call for external help.

If ever an expedition suffered from Murphy's Law, this was it. If a thing could go wrong, it did. Among several major miscalculations, the most fatal were Kennedy's decisions on air support for the rebels. He authorised an initial raid designed to eliminate Castro's own air force: it did not succeed completely, and his inhibitions about the international implications deterred him from permitting a second attack. He also accepted advice that jet trainer planes supplied earlier by the USA to the Cuban dictator Batista would not be effective in combat: Castro had meanwhile armed them, and they could out-manoeuvre the rebel aircraft.

Castro ordered the pilots of three of the handful of planes that he could still deploy to attack the enemy ships in the Bay of Pigs. They did so to such effect that only one battalion of the rebel brigade disembarked successfully; many of the other troops, and the CIA command post, never landed, and those on the beaches were left dreadfully short of supplies, fuel and ammunition.

The *Bahia de Cochinos* is readily noticeable on the map as a long, sharp inlet on the south coast of Matanzas Province, 60 miles south-east of Havana. Yet the name Bay of Pigs is given curiously little prominence in Cuban history and symbolism, and in the numerous Fidelist slogans that refer to the events of 1961. The universal term there for the entire episode is *Playa Girón*, the beach by the small village of that name, and the southern of the two where the invaders landed (a third landing was intended, but never achieved). The engagements around Playa Larga, at the northern end of the inlet, were equally decisive in the rout of the anti-Castro forces, but Girón is, unmistakably, the name of a place, whereas Cuba has many a 'Long Beach'.

*   *   *

Our quest for the *Tocororo* required careful preparation. After prolonged negotiations with several Ministries conducted by Rosa Salinas and other pillars of our locally-engaged staff, we obtained official permission to visit the area in February 1988, with the services of an expert guide.

We were driven to Playa Larga by Joaquín, another stalwart. A trim, courteous walnut of a man, our *chófer* set about his duties with a deep seriousness; but he had – like so many Cubans – a rich sense of humour. A favourite Joaquín moment came very early in our time in Havana. We were to present the superannuated Embassy Daimler as a stylish addition to the City's Automobile Museum. It had been characteristically generous of my predecessor Robin Fearn to leave it for us to perform this hand-over. But when the day came Joaquín was so overcome with the emotions of the occasion that he took a devious route to the ceremony. Embassy colleagues, catching glimpses of the 'White Whale' as it meandered around Old Havana without getting closer to the Museum, fanned out desperately to wave Joaquín in to his destination.

A fact known only to Joaquín at that point was that he had given the Daimler only a few drops of petrol for its final journey. It thus pulled up beside the welcoming party with its last gasp, in all senses. Nothing seemed amiss as it stood in splendour, immaculate and gleaming white in the sunshine, during the oratory that followed from the Mayor of Havana (Dr Oscar Fernández Mell, later Ambassador in London), the City Historian (Professor Eusebio Leal) and myself. Joaquín remained profoundly moved, but did mercifully recover sufficiently to head off, with discreet but unmistakable gestures to me as the speeches droned to their conclusion, a suggestion that the party might take a ceremonial ride in the now lifeless machine. It was as we returned home in the replacement Jaguar that we first heard the nasal chuckle, of theatrical complicity, that Joaquín uttered at special moments.

Now, two years on, he drove us along the *Carretera Central*. This was intended as a motorway to run the length of Cuba. The project had been achieved only partially: one came suddenly on uncompleted sections, and the quality of the surface was erratic. The most dramatic features of the road were some of the prospective turnings off it: several of these had been abandoned less than half-completed, with the roadway suspended in mid-air, giving a chilling new meaning to the term flyover.

On arrival at our hotel in the *Zapata*, we met our guide, Rogelio – a gentle and charming man with an encyclopaedic knowledge of the area and its wildlife. Nor was this his only distinction: many years before, he had represented Cuba in the Davis Cup at tennis. A white Cuban, his hair was grey, but he retained the build of an athlete. The following morning, we set off early. Rogelio, aware that the *Tocororo* was my Holy Grail, promised that we would head for an area frequented by the national bird. We drove through flat, scrubby countryside, and continued on foot in thicker woodland. It was a bright day, and the breeze was strengthening. Rogelio listened intently, and confirmed that *Tocororos* were nearby. My heart pounded as we advanced cautiously.

Suddenly Rogelio's whole demeanour changed, from calm assurance to unfeigned excitement. He froze; then pointed slowly at a clump of quite light trees. There we saw an incongruously huge shape: it was the largest owl that I had ever seen. '*Siguapa,*' whispered Rogelio. Hasty reference to the indispensable James Bond revealed that it was a Stygian Owl – all 18 inches of it. A photograph was imperative. My fumbling with the tripod was not helped by Rogelio's incredulous comments that it was quite a rare bird, and that this was the first time that even he had had a good view of one perched in broad daylight. My picture of this mighty owl *(16)* is marred by the swaying of the relatively slender branch where he had chosen to perch, and the wind in the surrounding foliage, but I hope that his magnificence is nevertheless apparent.

After this experience, the *Tocororos* might have been an anti-climax for Rogelio. But he seemed to share our delight at seeing them. There were three pairs, quite close together. Trogons are reputed to sit calmly for substantial periods, and these certainly obliged. It was Holy Grail time, as we admired their brilliant colours and exotic tails as they perched in light cover against a cloudless sky.

It was all too much for the would-be photographer. I made elementary mistakes at a rate that would have brought the Bay of Pigs invasion to an even earlier and more ignominious end. Determined to obtain close-up views, I left the X2 extender on the lens, although I knew that this could have dire consequences for the depth of field. Emboldened by the birds sitting so tight, I moved ever closer until I was directly underneath them, catching them from unflattering angles, and with excesses of light and shade.

That evening, as I reflected on what I knew to have been a hopelessly clumsy performance, Rogelio said that he assumed that we had seen our fill of *Tocororos*. We would go to another area in the morning, where he promised us further riches. He specified other owls, and the endemic Fernandina's Flicker, a cinnamon-coloured woodpecker. He was also

16. *Almost too big for his branch: Stygian Owl* (Asio stygius), *Zapata Peninsula, 1988*

17. *A singular tail: Cuban Trogon* ('Tocororo') (Priotelus temnurus), *near Playa Girón, 1988*

very keen to show us a lagoon celebrated for Roseate Spoonbills and a wide range of waders. There would, he said, just be time to fit all this in to the two full days that remained.

Davina and Rogelio were aghast when I pleaded to return to the *Tocororos*. Not daring to own up fully to my ineptitude, I said I feared that the conditions had made for excessive contrasts in my shots: it was essential for me to do justice to the national bird. After much muttering with another, more shadowy figure who was evidently keeping an eye on us all, Rogelio reluctantly agreed that, if the morning dawned cloudy, we could very briefly revisit the *Tocororos*. Never have I prayed more fervently for an overcast day.

I did not deserve it, but the next morning saw the Zapata Peninsula shrouded in a light, uniformly grey mist, that was lifting only gradually. We hurried off to the previous day's location. The Stygian Owl had moved on. I was sent in to the *Tocororos'* habitat entirely alone. I advanced, with my heart in my mouth. There was no sign of the birds until one flew over me, back towards Davina and Rogelio. My spirits fell. But then the same bird flew back, heading for the perches of the previous day. When I arrived, three *Tocororos* were sitting there: one was eating what looked like a dark berry; another was preening; and the third sat placidly, surveying me with a bright brown eye as it offered a perfect profile.

There were no shadows and no wind; and I too was calmer as I set about the photography. I took a promising shot – and the bird promptly flew away. I tried to compose myself again, and to get a good view of the preening bird. It was partially obscured, and I was about to move – when the first *Tocororo* flew back in, alighting in exactly the same spot, showing me its other profile. It settled, as if posing for me. There could be no mistake this time – and so, mercifully, it proved *(15 and 17)*. The latter photograph gives a good view of the tip of the Cuban Trogon's tail. Professor Hilary Fry, the renowned ornithologist from whom I have learned so much, has remarked to me that "... this is not just a ragged-tailed individual – it's how socio-sexual evolution has 'designed' it. I can't think offhand of any other bird species worldwide with a tail remotely like it."

I returned with relief to Davina and Rogelio. He was pointing out to her the endemic Cuban Bullfinch (which is altogether blacker than the European bird). We hurled ourselves in to the rest of our programme. Rogelio's intimate knowledge was uncanny. He brought us cheek by jowl with a pair of Greater Antillean Nightjars, sleeping lengthways on a branch. We duly saw the beautiful Fernandina's Flicker, and towards the end of the day we were fortunate to see another endemic bird, the Cuban Screech-Owl, emerging from its hole *(18 and 19)*. Later we saw Roseate Spoonbills, Flamingos and other waders in surroundings that presaged our experiences in the Camargue.

Rogelio also showed us a pair of Bee Hummingbirds. With a length of only two and a half inches, the male – which is even smaller than the female – is claimed by Bond and others to be the smallest of all birds. I did take a photograph of one, but it sadly does not warrant reproduction here.

We left the Zapata area with a rich diversity of images in our minds. We had come in search of a beautiful bird, and had seen it, along with many other spectacular natural phenomena. While absorbed in these wonders, we could put to the back of our minds the fact that we were walking the beaches and tracks where such decisive engagements had occurred in 1961. Yet reminders of these were all around. We saw the coral reefs – they looked pretty unmistakable – that had been designated as 'seaweed' by CIA planners, with damaging consequences for the expedition's landing craft. We walked on both Playa Larga and Playa Girón, and saw some of the aircraft, lovingly preserved, whose role had been so critical. And we could not miss the huge billboard declaring: "PLAYA GIRON: FIRST GREAT DEFEAT OF IMPERIALISM IN LATIN AMERICA," between images of Fidel leaping from a tank, and a rebel ship sinking in flames.

Castro lost 161 men in that battle; 107 of the invaders were killed, and almost 1,200 taken prisoner. The consequences in the longer term were massive. Initially, Fidel Castro was not such a dedicated Communist as his brother Raúl, Che Guevara and other revolutionaries around him. But once the threat from the USA had been confirmed so unequivocally, little stood in the way of Cuba's wholehearted commitment to the Communist camp.

Moscow moved rapidly. The Soviet Union had provided Castro with

18 & 19. Time to go out: Cuban Screech-Owl (Otus lawrencii), *Zapata Peninsula, 1988*

enough tanks and other military equipment to arm the forces that repulsed the invasion, but their programme of military assistance was far from complete. They rapidly increased it, determined that the Communist beachhead in the back yard of the USA would never again be at such risk. In tandem with the military hardware came comprehensive measures of internal security, under "advice" from Moscow, which entailed universal surveillance and repression. This dreary apparatus remains in place.

Against this changed background, and with the new United States President put to shame over Cuba, Khrushchev felt free to exploit his new asset to the full. His miscalculations in carrying this to the point of stationing intermediate range missiles in Cuba, with nuclear warheads, and underestimating Kennedy's resolve, brought the USSR and the USA to the brink of world war in October 1962. The Cuban Missile Crisis thus flowed directly from the Bay of Pigs fiasco of the previous year.

The peaceful demeanour of the *Tocororos*, and their accessibility, brought solace from reflections on the brush with Armageddon that had derived from their very habitat. But dramas about the photographs remained in store. I took the precious negatives back to Britain when we returned on leave, and had a number of large prints made of the two best portraits of the bird. I grandly envisaged presenting these to Ministers and other senior figures in Cuba. This disgraceful hubris led to a nightmarish episode in which nemesis, in the form of Iberia airlines, struck on our return journey, causing the bag containing all that I had ever wanted to picture of the *Tocororo* to disappear somewhere between Heathrow, Madrid and Havana. At weekends, I abandoned the woodpeckers at Jibacoa, and concentrated desperately on Kafkaesque enquiries and searches of baggage carousels at José Martí airport that seemed doomed to be fruitless.

Then, one steamy weekend afternoon, when I was on the point of giving in to total frustration as I waded alone through piles of miscellaneous luggage, I literally stumbled upon the missing bag, with everything mercifully intact within. Together with my massive relief, I resolved to try to show rather more becoming modesty about the photographs. Needless to say, I was not very successful.

20. Inquisitive: Mexican Green Jay (Cyanacorax yncas), *Uxmal, Mexico, 1987.*

5

Making the most of Regional Conferences

A bonus of our job in Havana was inclusion in more than one of the FCO's periodic regional conferences for heads of mission: in 1987 we attended meetings of both the Caribbean and the Latin American groups, which were held respectively in Kingston, Jamaica and in Mexico City.

These get-togethers enable ministers and senior officials from London to discuss policy and welfare issues with the men and women on the spot, and to return with some first-hand impressions of the area. For the heads of mission, they provide welcome opportunities to connect directly with colleagues in neighbouring posts, and with authorities from home. The latter can all too easily come across as the Orwellian, impersonal 'they,' especially if one is serving in a small and remote mission. This was – as so often – a time of reform in our Service, and it was enlightening and reassuring to clear our minds in conversation with the authors of administrative circulars that could otherwise seem dense and daunting.

Most of the participants in the two conferences were already old friends of ours. The team from London included Humphrey Maud, who came to dispense financial expertise: this long-established mate is also an expert birdwatcher. Happily, the Minister of State presiding on both occasions was the admirable Baroness Young. I previously had the privilege of working closely with Janet Young when I was Head of the Department that, following the war in the South Atlantic in 1982, strove to repair the fabric of life in the Falkland Islands, and to restore some prospect of economic and other co-operation with Argentina. These goals were not easily compatible in the immediate aftermath of the conflict. Rightly, they attracted much Parliamentary interest, and they aroused their fair share of public controversy. Life was hectic; but it was greatly eased by Janet Young's calm and wise handling of our business. It was a joy to see her again. (Sadly, Janet died a few years ago; she remained a beacon of good sense throughout her public life).

On these occasions we generally tried to take a few days' local leave, and achieved happy trips that enabled us to see something of Jamaica, and the Yucatán region of Mexico. In Jamaica, the Blue Mountains are dramatically beautiful, and much of the other scenery superb. A good number of the local people were charming, and very entertaining. Discussion of cricket is a universal currency in Caribbean territories that were once British. Enthusiastic responses are virtually guaranteed, especially if one takes care to extol the skills of the appropriate local hero: Courtney Walsh in Jamaica, Brian Lara in Trinidad, Gary Sobers in Barbados, Vivian Richards in Antigua, and so on.

Relations were not always straightforward, however, with Jamaicans encountered around the place. Even with the most friendly groups, conversations could be marred when our interlocutors were so heavily under the influence of the ubiquitous 'ganja' as to be of limited coherence. Moreover, compared with the sunny disposition of the locals in other islands, notably Tobago, there was an unmistakable sense among Jamaicans of a brooding and resentful mood. For Davina and me, there was an even stronger contrast between the sullen attitudes of some Jamaicans and the spontaneous welcomes we found throughout Cuba; we speculated about the respective influences of political, ethnic and cultural factors in these neighbouring islands.

None of this weighed on us too heavily during a hilariously enjoyable trip along the north coast of Jamaica in the company of Martin Berthoud – then High Commissioner in Trinidad and Tobago – and his wife Marguerite. Both are keen birdwatchers. But we soon met up – totally by chance – with some of the extended Lawrence clan from Brookline, Massachusetts. This family, especially the late James Lawrence and his delightful son Eddie, have been close friends to three generations of Palmers, and we proceeded to pack so many social and festive items into our schedule that there was little time for more tranquil pursuits. We did visit a remarkable establishment above Montego Bay where the lady proprietor fed hummingbirds from her hand, including the spectacular Red-billed Streamertail, endemic to Jamaica; and we often enjoyed the chattering and the vivid colours of Saffron Finches *(21)*, successfully introduced to Jamaica from the South American mainland.

It was only when Davina and I made our way separately to Frenchman's Cove, on the north-east coast of Jamaica, that we brought any sustained concentration to watching birds, and even this was almost shamefully sybaritic. This was once a most luxurious hotel, patronised by personalities from Hollywood. The facilities were no longer in peak condition, by any means, but Frenchman's Cove remained a heavenly spot. Its accommodation consisted of spacious bungalows, quite widely separated in spectacular locations above a perfect little beach, at the mouth of a vigorous stream; one could swim in limpid pools of fresh water as well as in the Caribbean Sea. In the early morning and late evening, several species of herons and sandpipers fed along the banks of the stream. We could leave behind the popping fuses in our bungalow and stroll down to stalk the Little Blue Heron, in particular *(22)*.

I did not take my large lens to Jamaica. This proved a mistake and, when the Latin American Heads of Mission Conference was held in Mexico City some months later, we resolved to do better. We travelled back to Cuba via Mérida in the Yucatán peninsula, having done some research into the best combination of Mayan ruins and birdwatching. We chose Uxmal, having heard enthusiastic accounts of the birds there from Davina's sister Susan Harley and her husband Christopher. Like most advice from the Harleys – who are all expert travellers – this guidance served us well.

As an archaeological site, we found Uxmal as evocative as any of the other main pre-Columbian sites that we had visited, of which the Inca ruins in Peru and Bolivia, and those of the Aztecs near Mexico City, were the most memorable. Unlike much of the Yucatán, Uxmal has the added attraction of being hilly. The Mayas were less bloodthirsty people than the Aztecs; their city-states, which flourished between 300 and 1000 AD, lived by trade. But Uxmal in particular was chronically short of water. Accordingly, the intricate imagery in the ornate and impressively proportioned architecture there is largely dedicated to Chac, the Mayan rain god, whose mask protrudes from many facades and cornices. Huge real-life iguanas, three feet long, enhanced the effect of these figures by freezing in silhouettes alongside them.

The Harleys had assured us that the hotel which they had chosen would provide excellent viewing of brightly coloured birds, on the spot. This was particularly true of Mexican Green Jays, which frequented the wooded grounds of the hotel. These were prominent in the early morning routine, alongside several species of yellow-breasted flycatchers. The

21. Successfully introduced: Saffron Finch (Sicalis flaveola)*, near Montego Bay, Jamaica, 1987*

22. *Poised: Little Blue Heron* (Egretta caerulea)*, Frenchman's Cove, Jamaica 1987*

latter ranged in size from the Great Kiskadee down through the Tropical
Kingbird to the Social (or Vermilion-crowned) Flycatcher. I gave priority
to a close-up of one of the decorative tropical jays. They are themselves
quite bold – inquisitive, even – and the quest was achieved without great
difficulty *(20)*.

Rather more effort was required to obtain clear views of the various
woodpeckers that were drumming and calling in the same woods. I was
reasonably successful in photographing a Golden-fronted Woodpecker
(23) – akin to the West Indian Woodpecker, but with the colours reversed
in its wing feathers, and reputed to store food in crevices in tree trunks.
At one point this individual was working on the same tree as an Acorn
Woodpecker: this smaller, red-crowned species has the reputation for
being more confiding, but I could not follow it to its nest, as was possible
with the Golden-fronted. I regularly saw Acorn Woodpeckers in flight:
besides frequenting oak trees, they are adept at catching insects on the
wing.

As we walked towards the Maya ruins, we continued to marvel at
these brilliant representatives at Uxmal of our favourite family of birds,
the woodpeckers. I remarked that we had not yet seen a Lineated
Woodpecker, a large black and white bird with a prominent red crest that
was said to be quite common in the area. Approaching the Mayan site,
we noticed that one particularly green and healthy-looking tree stood out
in the generally dun and arid landscape.

"If I were a Lineated Woodpecker," I said idly, "I would look for
insects in that green tree."

Davina walked ahead while I put a new film in my camera. I next saw
her under the green tree – and she was beckoning urgently.

"I think you were right," she whispered as I stumbled to join her.

The bird was by now moving up the trunk. There was not time to set
up the tripod, and my efforts were further impaired by the dim light
within the canopy of the tree; this was an occasion when the thrill of
seeing the handsome bird outweighed any subsequent satisfaction from
indifferent photographs recording the moment. As we moved on to the
centre of Uxmal, we reflected that this fine bird's quest for nourishment
in the lone green tree seemed to symbolise the Mayas' tenacious struggle
for water.

23. *At home: Golden-fronted Woodpecker* (Centurus aurifons), *Uxmal, Mexico, 1987*

24. *Almond blossom – a nice snack: Alexandrine Parakeet* (Psittacula eupatria), *Villa Drusiana, Rome, 1993*

6

GREEN BIRDS OF ROME

There are some common misconceptions about diplomatic accreditation to the Vatican, notably that the work is concerned exclusively with church matters, and is therefore short of real political content and, unless one is deeply religious, rather dull. The reality in 1991-95 was the very reverse of that. There was a dimension that I had enjoyed in Havana and elsewhere, and was missing at the Holy See: commercial work, of which I can remember just one instance, when we were asked to pursue the possible supply of a "Popemobile" of British manufacture. But political work was plentiful, active and absorbing. Many of the issues did derive initially from spiritual or religious considerations. But Pope John Paul II was so energetic and tireless in his pursuit of freedom of worship and other human rights, especially when the problems arose from state atheism and ethnic aggression, that these themes soon gathered real political momentum and required action at that level.

The Pope's campaign to liberate Eastern Europe from the tyranny of Communist rule had begun in his native Poland – President Lech Walesa, formerly the leader of the fearlessly independent Polish trade union Solidarity, was a frequent visitor to St Peter's – and parallel movements had continued apace elsewhere in the crumbling Soviet empire. If we needed confirmation that we were to be in Rome during a dramatic period on this front, it came as we travelled to Rome in August 1991. Emerging from a tunnel between Bologna and Florence, we heard on our car radio the breaking news of the coup against Gorbachev that was put down by anti-Communist forces under Boris Yeltsin.

At first, we still had a colleague representing the Soviet Union at the Vatican. He was pleasant and informative. I was in conversation with him at a Reception later in 1991 when we were joined by the Yugoslav Ambassador. The latter looked sombre: Croatia and Slovenia were on the point of gaining independence from Federal Yugoslavia, and he feared – all too correctly – its further disintegration.

"You will perhaps remember me", he remarked, "as the last Ambassador of Yugoslavia here."

"That could well be so, my friend," said the Soviet colleague, "but you will remember me for more than that: I am not only the first Ambassador of the Soviet Union to the Holy See: I shall also be the last."

By the end of 1991, he had been proved correct. When the Soviet Union had ceased to exist, he remained at his post – as Ambassador of Russia.

These were historic times: but that did not make them straightforward, and Eastern Europe continued to occupy much of our attention. As the succession of crises and massacres racked the former Yugoslavia, John Paul II and his senior advisers charged NATO governments with indifference to the tragedies of the Balkans, which the Pope found all the more culpable in view of the Western nations' responsibilities as custodians of Christian traditions. The Vatican went on to argue that it was the right and duty of the international community to 'disarm aggression' – this doctrine of humanitarian intervention has since become more familiar, beyond the confines of Europe.

The Pope was highly critical of other Western international policies, as well as the ethical relativism and the greed of the developed world. He chided EU and NATO governments for being slow to provide economic assistance to the countries of the defunct Warsaw Pact. Further afield, the Vatican expressed dismay at the dilatory provision of aid to the victims of famine in Ethiopia and other natural disasters. The Pope's spiritual teachings on issues of life and population were also spilling over into secular arenas, notably the United Nations. His reiteration that artificial means of birth control were 'intrinsically evil' added fuel to controversies at the UN Conference on Population and Development in 1994.

On Northern Ireland, on the other hand, where the Pope also invoked moral and ethical dimensions, the Vatican line was in close accord with our own policy, and that of the Republic of Ireland. It was a pleasure for my Irish colleague and me to report to the Holy See on progress such as the Joint Declaration of December 1993.

Together with this role of conducting relations with the Vatican on political issues on which the Roman Catholic Church was active, we had the privilege of supporting the quest for ecumenical progress. We did this in tandem with the Anglican Centre in Rome, which takes the lead in dealings with the Vatican on ecclesiastical matters. For the Pope, the priority lay in restoring relations with the Orthodox Churches of Eastern Europe. The divides between the Eastern and Western Churches, and the Christian and Ottoman Empires, were glaring historical fault-lines in the region. The Serbian Orthodox Church was deeply suspicious of Rome (as was the Russian). Here again, political considerations and religious traditions were enmeshed.

It was not, meanwhile, a promising time for Anglicans searching for Christian unity, with the Church of England ordaining women priests for the first time in 1994. This had been identified some decades previously as a "grave obstacle" to full reconciliation with Rome. In the event, relations were not so seriously disrupted as the authors of newspaper headlines such as "Pew – What a Scorcher" might have imagined. In fact there were impressive reaffirmations of both Churches' resolve to continue the dialogue.

We had a good view of the fellowship and commitment of the Anglican/Roman Catholic International Commission, whose leaders were then Bishop (now Cardinal) Cormac Murphy O'Connor for the Roman Catholics and Bishop Mark Santer on the Anglican side, supported by Canon (now Bishop) Stephen Platten. Evenings in the company of these inspiring personalities were richly entertaining: they consistently enlivened our house with their wit, warmth and musical talents.

It was thus under an array of different headings that we were in contact with a range of impressive interlocutors at the Vatican. Many were Italian; but I also worked closely with very senior personalities in the Holy See from Australia, Nigeria, the USA, Ireland, France, Germany, Argentina and elsewhere. A feature common to them all was the spontaneity of their welcome, in their different styles: the Australian Cardinal Edward Cassidy, for example, would not enter into discussion of thorny issues of Christian Unity without first ensuring that we were both up to date on recent developments in cricket around the world.

Another common reaction before we set off was to find people supposing that we were ourselves Roman Catholics. This was certainly the case with many of our colleagues from EU and NATO nations (some, like Germany and the Netherlands, alternate between Catholic and Protestant Ambassadors). But the convention for Britain was that the Head of the Mission to the Holy See should be a member of one of the Churches – of England or Scotland – of HM The Queen, whom we were representing.

This made it all the more necessary, on several counts, for the Deputy Head of Mission to be a Roman Catholic; and I remain deeply in debt to Patrick McCormick and Frank Doherty for their wisdom, tact and patience in that capacity. Patricia Corby and the locally-employed team provided brilliant support for us all. David Ryan, our driver, son of an Englishman who married an Italian lady and settled in Perugia, was an outsize personality in every sense. Big Dave's wholehearted commitment to his task endeared him to us and our visitors. His passengers were also treated to a free flow of observations on life in general, enriched with a vocabulary of Dave's own coinage. He would sympathise with me for being in a "quandarium", for example, and one of our regular collection points, the Keats/Shelley Museum in the Piazza di Spagna, was attributed by Dave to the hitherto undiscovered poet "Keith Shelley".

A theme already current even in the early 1990s was for the media to dwell on the Pope's physical frailty. For me, his resilience and fortitude were altogether more remarkable. He had grown up under severe conditions, when Poland was under Nazi and then Communist rule. In 1981, he was seriously wounded by three bullets from a would-be assassin. When we arrived ten years later, John Paul II – then aged 71 – was still regularly skiing on his winter holidays, and taking energetic mountain walks in summer. He had surgery in 1992 to remove an intestinal tumour; this was followed by a series of illnesses and injuries and, by the time we left in 1995, he was moving around with difficulty. Yet he appeared wholly undiminished in his mind, and in the warmth that he emanated. Personally, he was alert and genial, and fluent in numerous languages; in conversation, he was full of telling insights and endearingly avuncular asides.

John Paul II was to live for ten more years. After his death in April 2005, we learned that he had considered resigning in 2000, by which time he was severely afflicted by Parkinson's disease. But he was sustained by his exemplary resolve and above all by his belief – first expressed after the attempted assassination – that God alone would determine when his reign should end; and there is no doubt that spiritual as well as physical forces gave this Pope special levels of courage and endurance. There is paradox as one looks back over his 26 years as successor to St Peter. The man who did so much to liberate Catholics –

and others – from state atheism was sternly authoritarian in his own rule. He was an arch-conservative on many doctrinal issues, but his projection of the Papacy was radical: he made it visible globally – often dramatically so. Solidarity, his watchword in the early years in Poland, remained a central maxim and is, for me, the key to understanding him. For Karol Wojtyla, it evolved to mean the process whereby individual freedom must work for the common good, as opposed to the selfish consumerism which has been riding roughshod over the needs of the less privileged.

The Pope's standard greeting to me was: "How is your dear Queen?" The question manifestly came from the heart. When time permitted, he would revert to another matter that first arose in the unforgettable conversation – we were alone together for some 20 minutes – when I presented my credentials.

"You have the advantage over me of knowing Cuba," he then said with a smile, adding that he was trying hard to get there, and would go as soon as conditions were right – he was referring to the need for an acceptable level of religious freedom in Cuba. His visit finally took place in January 1998, by which time I had retired; but it was fascinating to hear about some of the labyrinthine negotiations between the Vatican and Havana that took place when we were in Rome.

It was during our time in Havana, in 1988, that John Paul II received his invitation from the Roman Catholic Bishops in Cuba. This followed the first in a series of visits by Cardinal Roger Etchegaray, President of the Pontifical Council for Justice and Peace, the Vatican's human rights arm. This formidable French Basque, with powers of endurance and resolve to match those of the Pope himself, was the ideal man to lead for the Holy See during the full decade of negotiations that ensued. On the Cuban side the amiable and competent Hermes Herrera, Vice-Minister of Culture while we were in Havana, appeared in Rome as their Ambassador to the Holy See.

The Pope's strategy of evangelisation faced different obstacles in Cuba to those in Eastern Europe. Even before the inroads of *santería*, the roots of the Roman Catholic Church in Cuba were nothing like as extensive as they were in other Latin American countries, let alone in the Pope's native Poland. Castro had attended schools in Santiago and

Havana run by Jesuits, and he claimed that his revolution was never anti-Catholic. For much of the time, it could afford not to be. But it was only in 1991 that it became possible for Christians to be Members of the Communist Party of Cuba; the Fidelist State was officially atheist until 1992, when it was declared "secular".

My contacts kept me generally aware of the roller-coaster nature of the exchanges between the Vatican and Havana. We read in *L'Osservatore Romano* in 1993 of the pastoral letter issued by the Cuban Bishops, deploring the sorry state of the island's economic, social and moral life. Undaunted by Cuban reactions to this, the Pope proceeded in the following year to appoint Archbishop Ortega of Havana a Cardinal. The negotiators for the Papal visit grappled over such matters as printing presses and visas for priests, and the arrangements for the people to see the Pope – in person and/or on television – when he did get to Cuba. I say 'when,' not 'if,' advisedly: from the Pope downwards, the Holy See appeared not to contemplate failure. Perhaps the Vatican negotiators were serenely aware that Castro's post-Cold War isolation had placed the ace of trumps in their hand. But I like to think that it was more than mere opportunism that impelled Fidel eventually to make the necessary concessions. I believe that these two outstanding figures realised that their meetings in Cuba could capture the imagination of the wider world at numerous other levels.

As the planning of the visit became more detailed, the head of the Pope's Press Office, Dr Joaquín Navarro Valls, joined in the negotiations. I always found this urbane and witty Spaniard to be an exceptionally effective operator. It is said that, when Navarro Valls called on Castro in Havana in 1997, Fidel immediately demanded "Tell me about the Pope".

"Mr President," replied the papal spokesman, "I envy you." Castro asked why.

"Because," Navarro Valls answered, "the Pope is praying for you every day – praying that a man with your formation will find his way back to God."

For once, Fidel Castro was silent.

*   *   *

We were lucky enough to live in a scenically and historically

25. *Caterpillar for the brood: Penduline Tit* (Remiz pendulinus), *Almone Valley, Rome, 1993*

atmospheric part of Rome. Our house, the Villa Drusiana, lay in the middle of the wedge of green that starts by the Tiber and extends out to the south-east of the city, through the Circus Maximus, the baths of Caracalla, the Catacombs and the golf course of Acqua Santa, on to the old *campagna*. The road through its centre is the Old Appian Way, first completed in 312 BC; it once ran all the way to Brindisi. Parts of it are still paved with the original huge lava blocks from the nearby Alban Hills. This area retains some of the farms and country lanes that used to surround Rome; it is full of relics and monuments evoking ages where ancient history merges into legend and myth.

This magical environment is also eminently bird-friendly. The Nightingales there were the only ones in my experience to be prominently visible while singing. In summer, warblers abound, including the Dartford and the Great Reed Warbler. Penduline Tits construct their hanging, purse-like nests above the brooks: I got a shot of one feeding a juicy caterpillar to its young *(25)*. These industrious little birds are common enough in Eastern Europe, but few are found to the west of Italy. In winter, there are flocks of finches in the fields around Rome, sometimes accompanied by Redstarts. Not all the warblers depart: the superbly melodious Blackcap and the distinctive Sardinian Warbler continued to delight us in our own garden. In our umbrella pines, tiny Treecreepers, Goldcrests and Firecrests were often busy.

One evening in spring, we were admiring from our garden the aerobatics of swifts and other recently arrived migrants: among these we caught the occasional flash of the brilliant hues of the European Bee-eater, and heard its distinctive liquid *pruuip* call. We marked the direction in which the birds headed at the end of the evening, and later went out to discover that they were nesting in the Almone Valley, still only four miles from the start of the green wedge. There were signs of nests from previous years. The birds' summer home was opposite the solitary little church of Sant' Urbano, originally a second century temple, and near to the spring of the Grotto of Egeria and the Sacred Wood, which both have legendary connections with Numa Pompilius, successor of Romulus. All of this lay in an enclave amid the sprawl of contemporary Rome.

26. *A bird of the sun: European Bee-eater* (Merops apiaster), *Almone Valley, Rome, 1994*

The Almone looks a modest stream, but it supports vigorous insect life, and its resident Bee-eater colony of around a dozen birds was regularly augmented by visitors from neighbouring territories. The resident birds burrowed out their nests along tunnels in low cliffs of sandy soil, whence they would emerge to perch on bare branches alongside the stream, and to swoop with grace and dexterity on dragonflies, moths and other insects. We marvelled at these manoeuvres, and at the distances covered by the European Bee-eater in its annual migrations: one bird, ringed near Moscow, was found 20 months later 5,000 miles away in Zimbabwe. The species is one of those that pair off for life; another endearing feature is that as many as 20% of the pairs have an unpaired male bird helping to bring food to the nest.

Besides their wonderful colouring that evokes sunny climes, Bee-eaters are a good prospect for a photographer, especially if one observes them quite soon after their arrival from Africa – the Rome birds were not particularly shy. Like flycatchers, Bee-eaters perch in the open to see their prey. After a season or two, I managed some decent close-ups of birds in the Almone valley (26), though I did not succeed in my ultimate goal of catching one in profile against the sky.

One summer evening, as we were setting off in search of further sightings of Bee-eaters, a green bird flew above the narrow lane from one umbrella pine tree to another. Having never seen a Bee-eater in a pine tree, we stopped to investigate. Scrutiny of the pines confirmed our sighting of a green bird – and another, and another. But these were not Bee-eaters: half a dozen medium-sized parakeets were cavorting noisily around the trees, their strong bills put to nimble use as they scrambled between the branches.

Within a few days we found that a colony of these birds was living in a large communal nest high up in a cedar tree in a suburban garden in the Via della Caffarella, part of a smart suburb of Rome to the north-east of the Almone Valley. The nest, built of twigs, was a good ten feet across; and the parakeets' principal activity was to enlarge it further. They flew in with sizeable twigs, sometimes almost small branches, which they carried in longitudinally in their claws. On landing, the precious building material was transferred to the bearer's bill for the bird's final waddle, or flop, onto the nest itself. All this was accompanied by great screeching

27. Construction material: Monk Parakeet (Myopsitta monachus), *Villa Drusiana, Rome, 1993*

28. In the main communal nest: Monk Parakeet, Via della Caffarella, Rome, 1993

29 & 30. Visiting: Blue-fronted Amazon (Amazona aestiva) *approaches the Monk Parakeets' communal nest, Via della Caffarella, Rome, 1994*

from the flock; the unrestrained vocalising continued as the twigs were painstakingly woven into the nest *(27 and 28)*.

The nest provided the key to the identification of these birds. An Argentine friend, familiar with them in his homeland, told us of the habits of the Monk Parakeet, including the Herculean labour of communal construction. Most other species of parakeet nest in holes in trees. Flailing through every bird book that I could lay my hands on, I found that the Monk Parakeet answered the description of our local flock in every other detail. Enquiries in the area revealed that a single pair had appeared some five years previously, and had steadily multiplied.

Some confusion developed when we saw a much larger parakeet, with a bright red bill and some rose-pink patches on his green plumage, near the Monks' dwelling. This proved to be a single male Alexandrine Parakeet – a bird native to South Asia. The Monks tolerated him in some circumstances; on foraging expeditions they may even have welcomed his formidable presence in deterring competitors. But any attempt by the Alexandrine to enter the Monks' nest provoked dire reactions: they drove him away, amid falling twigs and correspondingly extreme sound effects.

The tale of the parakeets became stranger still later in the year, when we saw several Monks bearing twigs into the heart of a palm tree near the front gate of our house – about a mile from the original nest. A breakaway group of some four pairs duly established themselves there: I could watch their construction work from the balcony of my dressing room. This development also led to the Alexandrine appearing more regularly in our garden and helping himself to almond blossom *(24)*. The bird's size – it is four inches longer – and the pink wing patches distinguish it from the Rose-ringed Parakeet, another South Asian species, of which thousands have established themselves in suburban Surrey. We occasionally saw a Rose-ringed individual in Rome. (Since returning home to Buckinghamshire, I have seen several at Eton and elsewhere in the Home Counties).

The party in the Via della Caffarella, and our garden, became even more varied with the arrival in our area of a Blue-fronted Amazon Parrot *(29)*, who also tried his luck at the Monk Parakeets' main nest *(30)*. I find it heartening as well as exotic that all these feral parrots and parakeets seem to be doing so well in Western Europe (Monk Parakeets have also

31. In one of our orange trees: juvenile Monk Parakeet (Myopsitta monachus*), Villa Drusiana, Rome, 1993*

established colonies across the USA). By hanging around the Monks' communal nests, the solitary Alexandrine and Blue-fronted Amazon were presumably yearning from time to time for the family dimension, but they were spared its rigours (that is a purely ornithological remark). In general, however, their behaviour was the very reverse of distressed. Above all, of course, they are free – for they must all be escaped birds, or their descendants.

Roman winters can become quite severely cold. My initial concern that the feral birds would suffer in the low temperatures was allayed, for the parakeets at any rate, when I learned that the native habitat of the Monk Parakeet includes the foothills of the Andes, and that Alexandrine and Rose-ringed Parakeets are seen close to the Himalayas. The established flocks have evidently been equally successful in dealing with threats from raptors and other predators. Moreover, while humans treat these birds as serious pests in Argentina and India respectively, on account of the damage they inflict on crops and fruit, the parakeets have not – yet! – acquired that stigma in Europe.

Our Italian neighbours, whose sleeping quarters were closer than ours to the palm in question, were understandably less amused than we were by the establishment of the new – and very noisy – colony of Monk Parakeets. Fortunately, they enjoyed the whole spectacle sufficiently to agree to leave the birds alone until they had raised one further generation; the juvenile birds were tamer, with engaging habits *(31 and 32)*. Only then did the neighbours send in their gardener to strip off the outer fronds of the palm. Our lodgers returned without too much ado to the Via della Caffarella, where another subsidiary nest soon took shape.

The villa in whose garden the Monk Parakeets were thus concentrated doubled as an outlet and warehouse for the clothing retailers Balloon, who specialised in imports from the Far East. The owners of this business used the villa for office purposes only, leaving Filipino staff in residence. All concerned at Balloon were genially tolerant of our obsessive interest in the parakeets, including the erection of tripods in their garden. We did our best to repay their kindness by encouraging the visitors whom we brought to see the birds to avail themselves of the opportunity for some bargain purchases of Balloon merchandise, in which we set an energetic example ourselves.

32. Playful: juvenile Monk Parakeets, Via della Caffarella, Rome, 1994

33. Spirited Royal Visitor, with friend: HRH Princess Margaret in the Piazza Navona, Rome, 1994

A detour to Balloon became a standard item in our itinerary for house guests of all levels. These included HRH Princess Margaret, who entered in to the spirit of this part of her visit (and its more formal features) with delightful enthusiasm. The following day, seeing a selection of large balloons for sale in the Piazza Navona, the Princess despatched me to buy one for her in the shape of a parrot*(33)*: this remained attached to the wrist of Her Royal Highness throughout several subsequent items on her programme.

Princess Margaret's visit was not without its challenging features, sometimes literally. At the end of the first day, the Princess handed me the Times, neatly folded to show the crossword: she had completed two thirds of it.

"Let's see what your Foreign Office brain can do with this," she said.

It was not so much brainpower as a surge of adrenaline that propelled me as I managed – unusually for me – to finish the puzzle. I then left it outside the Royal visitor's room. My reward came the following evening, when Princess Margaret suggested that we might attempt that day's crossword together. This was a joyous experience for me, as she drew on her impressive erudition and, most memorably, her lively wit; I was left with a suspicion that, the previous evening, Her Royal Highness had left only the easier clues for me.

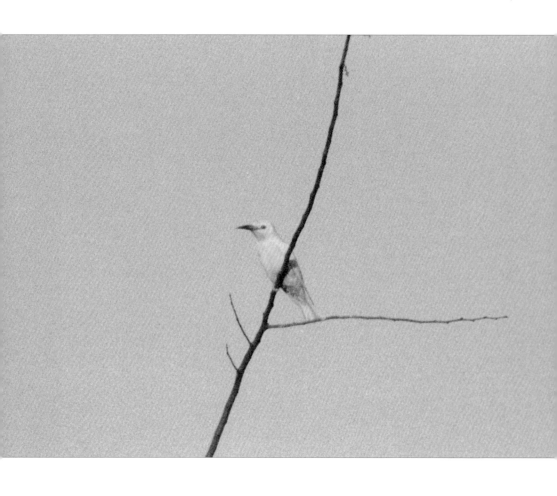

34. Rarity: Albino European Bee-eater (Merops apiaster), *Almone Valley, Rome, 1994*

36. *With prey: Albino European Bee-eater, Almone Valley, Rome, 1994*

like a Bee-eater's, yellow. Its shape, size and behaviour were identical to those of the normally coloured juveniles in its group, not least when wheeling and swooping close to the ground for its prey. (The European Bee-eater is also adept in its hunting at higher altitudes, suddenly twisting and dashing as it catches small flying insects – this was how we had first seen them from the house).

I managed to take some photographs *(34 and 35)* showing the white bird alone, and in close company with a normal juvenile. The adults in the valley also accepted it as a regular member of the group; it hunted and ate similar insects *(36)*. It could only be a European Bee-eater that had, unaccountably, grown white feathers.

This called for research, and I turned to the authoritative work "The Bee-eaters", by Professor Hilary Fry, which had already provided us with much fascinating information about the 24 species of bee-eaters around the world, and great enjoyment. I read with excitement in Professor Fry's Appendix on Aberrant Plumages that albinism was so rare among bee-eaters that he knew of only six instances at the time of writing. Moreover, most of these were only partially white: the exception was a skin of a Little Green Bee-eater in the British Museum that was pure creamy white apart from a yellow throat, and some green or brown washes elsewhere.

After leaving Rome in 1995, I had the pleasure of consulting Hilary Fry personally about our sightings. He is a charmingly accessible expert (who has since completed the definitive, seven-volume work *The Birds of Africa*, following many other distinguished works of ornithology that he has written). Having seen the photographs, Hilary confirmed that it was indeed a juvenile European Bee-eater. He then very kindly master-minded an article that appeared as a Note under my name entitled "Albino Bee-eater" in *British Birds* of 7 July 1997. The accompanying editorial comment remarked that such aberrations were certainly rare among birds in the Family Meropidae, adding that '. . . microscopical examination of individual feathers is required to establish the cause(s) of abnormal colouring in any single instance.' My first, and facetious, reaction was that it was a bit late to return to the Almone in search of a feather moulted by our albino, which had not, sadly, reappeared the following year. It then dawned on me that I could – in fact, should –

have looked for a feather at the time when I saw and photographed the bird.

If I needed any reminding of my status as a total amateur, and a beginner at that, this episode provided it. It was also a further instance of the kindness and patience shown to me consistently by expert ornithologists, whether in correspondence, or in casual meetings in the countryside. They seem genuinely to want others to share the full delight and excitement of their own experience: it is a matter of camaraderie, as opposed to competition. I am invariably cheered when I come across this wholesome and generous approach.

I am not, however, inclined to keep a huge list of all the birds that I have ever seen. For contemporary British 'twitchers' there is an elite '400 Club': to become a member, it is necessary to have seen 400 species of bird in our home islands alone. Some carry the process to more frenetic levels by engaging in 'races' to see the most species in a day. Then there are the formidable 'world listers', some of whose totals may approach half of the 10,000 species so far discovered.

While admiring the listers' diligence, I settle for jotting the briefest of notes in my various guide books to the birds of Britain, Europe, Cuba, Costa Rica, and so on, recording the place and date of my first sighting of a bird. I add details of subsequent encounters that have some unusual or interesting feature.

Hilary Fry's remarks in the first paragraph of his Preface are illuminating in the context of the human categories discussed here. I suspect that he is not the only ornithologist who is happy to be thought of also as a birdwatcher, but who would shy away from the label 'twitcher'. The competitive dimension that he notes is far removed from the pleasures of low-key watching of birds in the field that provide such rewarding fulfilment for expert and amateur alike.

This thought reinforces my preference for enjoying birds – 'ordinary', 'special' or whatever – as they occur, and for reserving my energy for the photography. For all the imperfections of my pictures of the albino Bee-eater, I hope that the capture of some images of this amazing creature is a modest justification of my approach. If not – well, as my revered Ambassador Edward Tomkins used to remark in other contexts in Paris, "the point is, Andrew, it doesn't matter."

37. Good camouflage: Hoopoe (Upupa epops) *at its nest in the Aurelian Wall, Villa Drusiana, Rome, 1994*

Rome has been a walled city since its earliest beginnings on the Palatine Hill, traditionally in the eighth century BC. Other walls followed as Rome expanded; and it is the Aurelian Wall that survives largely intact to this day. Many suppose, quite reasonably, that it owes its name to the great emperor Marcus Aurelius, who ruled from 161-180 AD; but it was in fact built a century after his time, under the emperors Aurelian (270-275 AD) and Probus (276-282), and is named after the first of these.

The Aurelian Wall was completed in 278 AD, extending for 12 miles round, with 18 main gates – many still in use – and 381 towers; it took in all the Seven Hills of Rome. Aurelian had recently defeated the Alemanii, and built the wall with the aim of repelling further Barbarian invaders. It was strengthened in the fourth and fifth centuries (this did not prevent Rome from being sacked by the Goths in 410).

The same wall remained the basic defensive shield of the city for many centuries thereafter. The army of the nascent Kingdom of Italy needed to breach it with artillery in 1870 in the attack that was so decisive in the unification of the country. This was made near the Porta Pia, beside what is now the Residence of our colleague the French Ambassador to the Holy See, and not far along the Aurelian Wall from the offices of our own Embassy to the Republic of Italy.

A section of the Aurelian Wall faced our house, across the lawn: we had a garden wall unlike any other. Each morning, before setting off for the office, I walked along the path beneath the wall, accompanied by my rather unusual dogs, led by Guagua (pronounced 'wawa' – the word is a Cuban endearment meaning 'sweet little thing'). This delicately corgi-esque mongrel had on her own initiative arrived in our household in Havana as a young stray. She was an exceptionally engaging and resolute personality. She was duly joined by Basil and Mini, two of her offspring from a Roman liaison that was entirely of her own choosing, after she had rejected prospective pedigree suitors. (This pair turned 12 years of age in October 2004, and sprawl loyally beside me as I write; Guagua eventually joined the mongrels in the sky in 2003, at the fine age of 17). With this trio around me, I would look through the narrow vents at the outline of the Alban Hills, or along the wall to the towers of the Porta San Sebastiano, so impressively castellated by the sixth century emperor Belisarius. The sense of history was as powerful there as anywhere in Rome.

Moments later, waiting in the rush-hour to pass through the Gate of St Sebastian on my way to work, I could banish the noise and fumes from my mind and visualise some of the emperors in triumphal procession, or martyrs and slaves in less happy circumstances. Over many centuries, continuous and immensely varied traffic had passed along the Via Appia Antica and through what became "our" gate, as we were privileged to regard it, in the great Aurelian Wall.

The Wall has sundry holes and crevices that formerly bore the beams and other structures of its fortifications, once manned by legionaries. Some of these inlets now provide convenient nesting sites for birds. Each year, a new brood of Little Owls appeared in and around our garden, and we were pleasantly aware in all seasons of their presence in the wall. This species is diurnal as well as nocturnal, and it was not uncommon to find oneself under scrutiny from a Little Owl perched in the wall or in an Umbrella Pine tree *(38 and 39)*.

Their most engaging behaviour *en famille* occurred by night, however. The garden was floodlit by security lights, which attracted large numbers of moths and other insects – juicy snacks for the adult owls to feed to their demanding young. We heard the importunate hissing of the juveniles as they sat in the olive trees under the Aurelian Wall just after dusk, urging their parents to bring them a moth or a cricket. After a few evenings of this, the adults forced the young to fend for themselves, and we were privileged witnesses as they worked on their hunting skills on the grass immediately outside our dining room window.

It was possible, by sitting quietly on our terrace, to get an even closer view of the Little Owls at this stage in their development. They once provided a particularly spectacular evening show for Ray Flynn, the United States Ambassador, and his family. It had been agreed that we would not invite anyone else, and Davina and I feared that the Flynns' teenage daughters might find the evening boring, but the Little Owls made it memorable for us all: it was as if our respective family circles were overlapping.

Neighbours a short way along the wall told us of sightings of the Scops Owl – even smaller than the Little Owl, and less commonly

38 & 39. You are being watched: Little Owl (Athene noctua), *Villa Drusiana, Rome, 1995*

seen. It has a distinctive mewing call, but paid us only occasional visits: I believe that our Little Owls were jealous guardians of their territory.

In summer, Spotted Flycatchers were active in the garden, which they approached from the direction of the Wall: I am sure that they nested in it. They perched on our citrus trees *(40)* before flying out to snap up insects.

Hoopoes were also regular summer visitors to our garden. Most of the books on birds of Britain and Europe show, towards the middle of the work, a sequence of outstandingly colourful birds: the Bee-eater, the Roller, the Hoopoe and the Kingfisher – each a strong contender for Holy Grail status. I had never before got at all close to a Hoopoe. The first sign of their presence was usually a series of fearful screeches as new arrivals disputed the choice nesting sites. Once established, they uttered the more mellifluous 'poop-poop-poop' from which their name derives. For the most part this is a dove-like coo, but can also come across as a distant bark. Hoopoes are said generally to prefer to nest in holes in trees, but the crannies in our section of the Aurelian Wall appealed to successive pairs.

We wondered for how many centuries Hoopoes had been arriving from Tunisia or elsewhere in Africa to raise their broods in such historic locations. These decorative birds are well represented in Renaissance art. Each time I called on the Papal Secretariat of State, I would pass through the Loggia of Raphael on the second floor of the Courtyard of St Damasus at the Vatican. The paintings on the vaults and borders of this breathtaking gallery include wonderfully lifelike images of birds and other creatures; whatever the urgency of my business, I invariably gazed up at a beautiful sixteenth century image of a Hoopoe (probably by Giovanni da Udine), and felt all the better for it.

On summer evenings, as the parent Hoopoes brought caterpillars and other titbits to their nestlings, I would creep around at a respectful distance and try to catch an image of the birds in profile. One year, they chose a nesting hole with a very small aperture, which was of great help as I locked on with the tripod and sought to perfect the focus *(37)*.

To the photographer, there is irony – disappointment, even – when a bird whose markings make it stand out against a normal green background appears camouflaged against the Wall, and there was no means of taking its picture from a different angle. But the value of this camouflage, especially for the newly-emerged young Hoopoes, could well have been an important factor in bringing these splendid birds to the Aurelian Wall in the first place, whenever they started to frequent it; and we were duly thankful for this further enhancement of our Roman summers.

40. Prominent perch: Spotted Flycatcher (Musicapa striata), *Villa Drusiana, Rome, 1993*

41. *Hungry for ants: Green Woodpecker* (Picus Viridis), *Little Missenden, 1996*

9   THRILLS AND SPILLS OF "RETIREMENT"

I retired from the Diplomatic Service in 1996. The Service has a statutory retirement age of 60. This has several merits. It clears the way for postings, like our own to Havana, where relative youth and vigour can be assets in a Head of Mission. It also means that, on retiring, we retain – in theory at least – sufficient vitality to perform energetically in a new career. The downside is that it deprives the Service of the wise inputs of those who are still at their peak at the age of 60.

Either way, 'retired but not inactive' was the maxim for the years ahead. I soon received help from exalted levels. His Royal Highness the Duke of Kent, for whom I had worked as Private Secretary from 1988 to 1990, kindly took me back in to his Household as one of his Extra Equerries, alongside another former Private Secretary, the long-serving Sir Richard Buckley – an exceptionally shrewd and genial friend. The duties are not full-time, but the exemplary standards of the Duke himself and the good fellowship of the office run by his present Private Secretary, Nick Adamson, engender strong and continuing bonds throughout the team.

Later in 1996 Lord Carrington, in his capacity as Chairman of the Bilderberg Meetings, recruited me as the Local Organiser of the 1998 meeting, which was due to be held in Britain. I reported directly to him and to Andrew Knight, Kenneth Clarke and Martin Taylor, who were the UK Members of the Steering Committee – and all, of course, very high achievers in other fields. Ken Clarke is another keen and convivial birdwatcher.

I first met Lord Carrington when, as Foreign Secretary, he accompanied The Queen on her State visit to Norway in 1981. He flew in separately, as he had been attending a NATO ministerial meeting. I did not catch up with him until the King of Norway's state banquet.

"Secretary of State," I gushed, "I'm sorry that I couldn't be at the airport to meet you."

"No you're not," Lord Carrington replied with a friendly prod at my stiff evening shirt, "or you certainly shouldn't be, anyway – airports are such ghastly places."

This was an illuminating introduction to the Carrington style, simultaneously deflating pomposity, setting people at ease and encouraging them to concentrate on essentials.

The following year, when I was returning to Oslo a few days ahead of Davina after a spell of leave, I learned on my car radio as I disembarked from the ferry that Lord Carrington had resigned as Foreign Secretary following the Argentine invasion of the Falkland Islands. It was a step for which he still receives warm praise – and rightly so. At the time, I was too devastated to continue my journey: for quite a while, I sat in my car at the dockside, feeling utterly bereft. Any opportunity to work for him in another arena was thus doubly welcome. Moreover, he has since been unable to escape from me, for he is Chancellor of the University of Reading, where I have been a member of the Council since 1996. Peter and Iona Carrington provide exemplary leadership there, and are as respected and popular as they were at the FCO.

The Bilderberg Meetings date from 1954. They are a wholly independent organisation, which grew from the concern of the late Prince Bernhard of the Netherlands, among others, that the industrialised democracies on both sides of the Atlantic were not working together as they should on matters of critical importance. To help correct this, Bilderberg meetings have from the outset been private, in order to encourage frank and open discussion.

Each year, the main conference is held in a different country; it was Britain's turn in 1998, and the first decision required was the venue. In consultation with Maja Banck, the formidably efficient anchor-person for Bilderberg, we chose the Turnberry Hotel in Ayrshire. This long, white and imposing Edwardian building, overlooking Ailsa Craig and the Isle of Arran, is best known as a golfing shrine. The Manager there, Ross Furlong, was first class from the initial reconnaissance to the final clear-up, and we soon became good friends.

Another early move was the appointment of Mike Goddard as my deputy. I already knew this large and amiable Londoner when he worked for Andrew Knight while the latter was still based in London. I do not know whether Mike would say the same, but for me working in tandem with him was an optimal arrangement. He was good-humoured and unflappable throughout, and we saw eye to eye on all aspects of the Bilderberg meeting, not to mention such strategic themes as football and music – an encyclopaedic knowledge of the former is as valuable in

Scotland as it is in Italy. We were later joined by Julie Stamm and Felicity Chudley, who were both brilliant and heroic.

The preparatory work for Turnberry entailed very thorough liaison with the admirably efficient Strathclyde Police. This went into minute detail with such intensity that occasional misunderstandings were perhaps inevitable; I readily accept personal responsibility for the majority of such *contretemps*. We also worked very closely with the authorities at Glasgow and Prestwick Airports, and with providers of cars, marquees, sound systems and all manner of other conference facilities. I attended the 1997 Bilderberg meeting in the USA, which was held near Atlanta: this gave me invaluable experience, and enabled me to work alongside key members of Maja Banck's staff from Amsterdam.

Sometimes we needed the Carrington touch to restore perspective, as in the case of the allocation of rooms in the Turnberry Hotel. It was feared that participants given the view of the rolling Ayrshire countryside would regard themselves as second-class citizens compared to those who could survey the famous links and the sea and islands beyond.

"You can certainly put me down for the inland view, for a start," declared our Chairman on hearing of these concerns, adding that he had already had his fill of the view over Ailsa Craig (Lord Carrington's *ipsissima verba* were "that boring rock").

At both the 1997 and 1998 conferences a degree of anxiety was generated under the related headings of publicity – or rather the lack of it – and security. A full list of the 120 participants, described in the press release as a "broad cross-section of leading citizens, in and out of government", was issued as the meetings began. (The 1997 participants included a sparkling Hillary Clinton). But, apart from re-emphasising the flexibility and informality of the Bilderberg forum, and making it clear that no resolutions were proposed and no policy statements issued on these occasions, the central Bilderberg staff saw to it that the press releases gave no other details.

Some observers chose to interpret the bland formulations of this minimalist presentation as a smokescreen for Machiavellian intrigues. If not altogether surprising, this was not wholly deserved for, in fact, the organisers' accounts of the Bilderberg process were absolutely accurate.

Moreover, as I was able to confirm at first hand, several of its chief merits did indeed derive from the privacy as well as the informality of its discussions. These covered such delicate – if predictable – areas as the crises in the Balkans; the future of the world's financial system; and the outlook for the European Union. It was natural for the contributions of the likes of George Robertson (then Secretary of State for Defence), Javier Solana (then Secretary-General of NATO) and James Wolfensohn (President of the World Bank) to be more imaginative if the speakers could be certain that their words would not reappear in the media. At the same time, the participants' wide diversity of background and viewpoint meant that they seldom agreed in their respective analyses of difficult issues in international politics or economics. They were thus hardly in a position to devise, still less implement, Machiavellian deals to solve them, even if they wished to do so.

Nevertheless, the conspiracy theorists insisted that the illustrious participants had met not only to plot the future course of world affairs, but to arrange secret dispositions to bring their schemes into effect. Not content with these wild allegations, some of the anti-Bilderberg brigade tried to infiltrate the meetings. At Turnberry, the ever-alert Strathclyde Police easily thwarted them, but they still sought to suborn hotel staff to hand over the contents of participants' waste paper baskets: behaviour every bit as underhand as the darkest suspicions that its perpetrators claimed to harbour of Bilderberg aspirations to "world government".

These tendencies produced comical media coverage – and some ashen faces among the conference organisers – as the Turnberry meeting approached. Headlines proclaimed that the "All-powerful Think-tank" was a "Secret Group that Rules the World". Colourful variations on the theme included "Movers and Shakers Settling Down for Kippergate Conspiracy" – an allusion revealing that someone had at least been prepared to answer questions about the menu for breakfast at Turnberry.

One of the most entertaining misperceptions appeared in a Sunday tabloid a whole year later. Under the headline "Are They Plotting To Rule The World?" five people are shown on the steps of the Turnberry Hotel; a caption describes them as "World Leaders". However, of the five, only two could ever qualify for that label: Lord Carrington himself and Leon

42. *How was it for you? Oystercatchers* (Haematopus ostralegus)*, Ayrshire, 1998*

(now Lord) Brittan. The remainder are the menial figures of the manager of the hotel, a security operative, and yours truly.

Another concern had been that, in inviting 120 great and good from around the world to the west of Scotland in mid-May, we were taking a risk with the weather. But our prayers were answered with cloudless skies and summer temperatures. Overall, a number of participants were kind enough to comment that the outcome of our preparations had been comparably sunny. This generosity was cheering, and consoling in my remorse at the Palmer own goals with the incomparable Strathclyde Police. As with other high-level occasions, selective recall can make the event seem far more entertaining than it appeared at the time; but I would not have missed the experience for anything.

When Mike and I had completed the post-conference work, I was available to spend more time at the University of Reading, where I had by this time been appointed to the Standing Committee of the Council and a number of other bodies.

*   *   *

The Ayrshire coast holds many birds, especially waders. I had very little time for watching them as the Bilderberg momentum developed but, thankfully, the chef at the Turnberry Hotel was as keen as myself, and marked my card accordingly. His generous and precise guidance enabled me to go straight to a couple of excellent sites, notably the estuary of the River Doon, below Robert Burns' cottage at Alloway, just south of Ayr.

After the conference was over, I was lucky in getting close to a pair of Oystercatchers as they sought a nesting site *(42)*. Unlike many of the other waders that I saw at Alloway, such as the Redshank and Turnstone, Oystercatchers are resident in Britain throughout the year. Nor is this most pleasing bird confined to the coast: especially in the north of Scotland, I have seen considerable numbers on inland fields, and by rivers. One nevertheless associates its piping, trilling voice primarily with the seashore, where it is audible across a great distance. At closer range, there is something agreeably confident – reassuring, even – about Oystercatchers' orange bills and bright gaze. The closest I ever came to

43. *Young, but with adult markings: Great Spotted Woodpecker* (Dendrocops major), *Little Missenden, 1996*
44. *Outstanding garden bird: Great Spotted Woodpecker, Little Missenden, 1997*

one was while swimming in Oslo Fjord, where the water can become really warm in summer. I reached a low rock, and was starting to climb out when an Oystercatcher suddenly appeared from the other side. Both parties withdrew quietly and, in my case, apologetically. In flight, too, these birds' smart markings as they skim the waves are an elegant feature of our beaches and cliffs; I find them evocative and delightful.

Since retiring from the Diplomatic Service, I have of course been able to spend more time in our garden in Buckinghamshire. Predictably, birds claim a high priority in my attention there. As modern farming methods have made fields and hedgerows less hospitable, several species have become more common in gardens. To my immense pleasure, this has applied to woodpeckers – both the Great Spotted and the Green. I have not yet succeeded, in Britain, in locking my lens on to activity at a woodpecker's nesting hole, as I was able to do in Cuba. But I have observed several in nearby Penn Wood, which the Woodland Trust has recently purchased, forestalling its threatened conversion into a golf course. In the garden, the tempo of the woodpeckers' visits rises when adult birds are escorting their fledglings on early sorties; I managed a decent shot of a juvenile Great Spotted Woodpecker in one of our apple trees *(43)*. They lose their red crowns as they mature: the adult male has a red nape *(44)*, and the adult female no red at all on her head.

The Green Woodpecker is larger than the Great Spotted, but by repu-tation more shy, so I expected greater difficulty in photographing them. The hot summers of the late 1990s came to my assistance, however. Green Woodpeckers are predominantly ground feeders, devouring large numbers of insects, with a strong preference for ants. When the countryside is hard and baked, such food is easier to find in gardens. One August, it was clear from the volume of the "yaffles" – the distinctive, accelerating "klew-klew-klew" laugh of the Green Woodpecker, so different from the succinct "chip" of the Great Spotted – that a pair of them was coming close to the house.

I concealed myself in a garden shed, and lightly watered an area of lawn in what seemed to be suitable range. After a few evenings of holing myself up in this way, and seeing the birds only at a distance, the thrilling moment came when one of them hopped closer and closer to my "hide". I did not then have autofocus, so operations became breathless as I strove

45. Handsome from all angles: Green Woodpecker (Picus viridis), *Little Missenden, 1996*

46. Still speckled: juvenile Green Woodpecker, Little Missenden, 1997

47. Now what are they up to? Lapwing (Vanellus vanellus), *Little Missenden, 1999*

to maintain alignment of the split-line image. I managed some shots *(41 and 45)*. The bird then came so close that I could hear its footsteps in the dry grass. Suddenly, I could no longer keep the focus, and it dawned on me that the Green Woodpecker was too near for clarity in the zoom lens: a problem that one should welcome, I suppose, and any lingering frustration was outweighed by the thrill of seeing this beautiful bird almost at my feet. He only turned away on reaching the paving stones immediately outside the shed; for once, my improvised – and some would say idle – attempt at concealment had been entirely successful.

A few days later, the same Green Woodpecker returned to the garden with one of its offspring in tow. Juveniles of this species *(46)* take longer than the young Great Spotted Woodpecker to develop plumage similar to their parents; it is usually autumn by the time that they resemble adults.

Another parental moment in our garden enabled me to get a close-up of a Lapwing *(47)* anxiously pursuing an errant juvenile. These handsome plumed plovers, widely known as 'pee-wits' from their call, have suffered seriously from agricultural changes in Britain. But the Royal Society for the Protection of Birds (RSPB), with co-operation from farmers, are now helping them to re-establish themselves, together with other farmland birds.

It is only a short walk from our village to Shardeloes. This huge and elegant house is now divided into apartments. It stands on a hill overlooking its park and a stretch of the Amersham bypass. I was once driving our younger son Michael home to Little Missenden along this road, for a day out from his preparatory school, accompanied by a couple of his friends.

"We are nearly there," I informed them.

"Gosh, Palmer," squeaked one of Michael's schoolmates, who came from a well-heeled family, "is that your house up there?"

An affirmative answer was clearly expected; our reply, to the effect that Michael's home had at least a hundred fewer rooms than Shardeloes, was met with silence as disappointed as it was unimpressed.

Shardeloes is also the home of Amersham Cricket Club, for whom the fully grown Michael Palmer later enjoyed playing. The estate includes a large lake, and is home to a good array of birds. There is usually a breeding pair of Great Crested Grebes on the lake in the early summer.

48. Off my back: Great Crested Grebes (Podiceps cristatus)*, Shardeloes, Amersham, 1989*

One evening, in days when I was moving more nimbly, I concealed myself in some reeds on the north bank of the lake, and observed the delightful spectacle of the adult birds carrying their chicks on their backs. The light was not right for photographs: I needed to return early in the morning, when the rising sun would be behind me.

I duly settled into the reeds before breakfast the following day. As the birds emerged from behind a willow branch, I felt the water of the lake enveloping my feet, soon followed by my ankles, knees . . . and higher still. The extra weight of my tripod and other equipment was causing me to submerge, none too gracefully. I just managed to keep the Crested Grebes in the viewfinder for half a dozen shots before withdrawing from what was fast becoming a cold and muddy dawn fiasco. It was only when I looked back at the birds from *terra firma* that I realised that the chicks were no longer riding on their parents' backs: instead, they were pursuing them *(48)*, indignantly pressing for what they regarded as their customary transportation, and meeting with firm rejection. The adults had provided security while the chicks were seriously vulnerable; it was now time for them to find their own way around.

The Grebes' dedicated but pragmatic "parenting" – another ugly verb recently forced into our vocabulary – prompted further comparisons with human attitudes, as I hurried home for a hot bath (in mid-morning, in June). However hard one should try to be "scientific" and avoid drawing such parallels, few would deny that family behaviour among these grebes, like the Cuban woodpeckers before them, provided some relevant hints for human parents and grandparents, as well as a good deal of harmless amusement.

49. Perfect profile: Greater Flamingo (Phoenicopterus ruber), *Etang du Fangassier, Camargue, 2003*

In the Provence region of France, just to the north of Arles, the mighty Rhône divides into two arms: the Grand Rhône, which reaches the Mediterranean Sea at Port-St-Louis, and the Petit Rhône, emerging some 14 miles further west at Les Saintes Maries-de-la-Mer. This delta is the heart of the Camargue, a spacious complex of wetlands and cultivated areas that provides a wide diversity of habitats: marshland, rice fields, lakes, brackish pools, saline lagoons, dunes and seashore. Distinctive black cattle and grey ponies roam alongside a rich variety of birds.

A number of our French friends speak with reverence of the Camargue, its National Park and its Zoological and Botanical Reserve. The Michelin Guide describes it as '. . . the most original and romantic region of Provence and possibly of France.' Some Britons, on the other hand, have dismissed it as empty and boring, their comments recalling the remark of a senior official from the Bank of England on a visit to Bolivia. I was enthusing to him about the glorious spectacle of the wide spaces of the *altiplano,* dominated on each side by the snowy peaks of the two *cordilleras* of the Andes.

"I suppose it's alright," he mused, "if you're looking for miles and miles of b****r all."

Without necessarily expressing it thus, many of us do find that broad, open spaces have an increasing appeal in today's congested world.

My appreciation of the Camargue developed gradually over the past 20 years. At first, we sought instant gratification, rushing round the Roman remains at Arles and dashing off a few photographs of bulls and Flamingos before continuing our journey down to the Var. It has proved infinitely more rewarding to spend some leisurely days around the coastal lagoons; we have found that, as one soaks up the atmosphere of the Camargue, its singular allure establishes itself.

Part of this appeal derives from awareness that the history of this part of Provence is exceptionally colourful. Both Marseilles and Arles were colonised by the Greeks. Under the Romans, Arles prospered – especially when Marseilles was punished by Julius Caesar for supporting Pompey against him. Arles was also favoured by the Emperor Constantine, following his conversion to Christianity. By the Middle Ages, the political status of Arles had declined by comparison with Aix, as well as

Marseilles; but the amphitheatre and other monuments still remind us of the times when Arles was a major political and religious centre.

Local rivalries are still deeply entrenched, and there is abundant historical confirmation of them. King Louis IX of France built the walled town of Aigues-Mortes as a base for the launching of the Seventh Crusade in 1248 because Marseilles was still a "foreign" port, ruled by the Counts of Provence; the town is still dominated by its ramparts and massive fortified tower. The exploits of Saint Louis – as the king became – are also evoked by the port bearing his name. Meanwhile, according to legend, Les Saintes Maries-de-la-Mer, which lies between Port-St-Louis and Aigues-Mortes, was the spot where Mary Magdalene and Mary the mother of James landed after being cast out to sea by the Jews of Jerusalem. Their relics and those of their black servant Sarah, enshrined in the large fortified church, inspire a large pilgrimage each spring.

Antiquity is not unchallenged, however. Looking east from the Camargue towards Marseilles, the flares and other oil installations of Fos are all too visible beyond the lagoons, the wading birds and the soaring Black Kites that are common at that end of the reserve. The natural landscape is also subject to change, such is the strength of the conflicting forces of, on the one hand, the Rhône and the Mistral that blows down it; and, on the other, the currents, storms and gales of the Mediterranean. The heavy alluvial deposits carried down the Rhône have caused the sea to recede in several places: Aigues Mortes ceased to be a port as early as the fourteenth century, and is now 15 kilometres inland. Les Saintes Maries-de-la-Mer, on the other hand, needs the protection of break-waters. The *Digue à la mer*, a sturdy dike, was built in the nineteenth century to provide shelter for the lagoons and lakes at the southern centre of the Camargue. Within it, and more widely, an elaborate system of pumps and sluices maintains the balance between the freshwater, brackish and saline zones.

For many people, the Greater Flamingo is the symbol of the Camargue, which includes the major breeding colony of this species in Europe, at the Etang du Fangassier. As many as 2,000-3,000 of these birds now winter in the Camargue, with several times that number coming north from the African shore of the Mediterranean to breed in the spring and summer.

50. & 51. S-bends and Mirror image: Greater Flamingos, Camargue, 2001 and 2004

The French call the birds *Flamants Roses*. In fact, they only become pink gradually, over a period of four to five years; juveniles remain completely grey until their second season. The colouring process is influenced by their food, which consists mainly of small invertebrates from the bed of shallow salt or brackish lagoons. The birds filter these tiny organisms through their bills, which they move in semicircles and then backwards, towards their feet, as they advance through their feeding grounds.

Even when they are fully-grown, the Flamingos' most spectacular plumage is only seen in flight, and on take-off and landing, when the striking carmine and black of their wing feathers emerge fully. This makes them, for me, at their most engaging as photographic targets when they are airborne. But much pleasure may still be had in observing and recording them as they stand in the water, especially when their reflections create precise mirror images in calm conditions *(51)*, or make a series of double S-bends with their necks *(50)*.

Initially, I found it hard to visualise these gangling apparitions achieving any sort of aerodynamic elegance. But a full day spent almost anywhere in the Camargue in early summer will demonstrate the grace and power of Flamingos in flight. Adult birds move about regularly as they alternate between tending their single chicks at the nesting colony at the Etang du Fangassier and their chosen feeding places, which can be some distance away. Many of them travel in sizeable groups of up to 40 or 50 birds. They arrange themselves in arrowhead formations, to reduce wind resistance, changing to straight lines ahead as they approach their destination. It is a breathtaking sight.

I have experimented with numerous locations in my quest for the perfect shot of Flamingos in the air. One should be prepared to see formations virtually at random in the mornings and evenings; if the sun catches them as they alter direction, it is definitely worth a picture *(52)*. The site at the Etang du Fangassier is, thankfully, well protected: one can just discern, as an indistinct pinkish line on the horizon, the island where the great colony establishes thousands of nests. But there is access to a broad, rough track running along the western shore of the lagoon, permitting very good viewing of arrivals and departures in the evenings. A preliminary assessment of wind direction and prevailing flight paths, followed by rudimentary concealment, or even refraining from sudden

52. Catching the evening sunlight: Greater Flamingos, Les Saintes Maries-de-la-Mer, 2003

sound or movement, should ensure that at least some of the formations pass excitingly close, enabling one to hear the heavy swish of their wing-beat. Always provided, of course, that one's human companions adopt the same approach.

One evening, a large camper-style vehicle bounced along the track and stopped a few yards away from us. It had Italian registration. Much as we love that country and its people, our hearts sank – and rightly so, for over a dozen occupants poured from it, each shouting louder than the next in vain attempts to make their respective points. (This is the acknowledged dynamic of the human decibel count in Italy). Pink arrowheads which had been heading towards us veered away to right and left. The Italians paid no attention. When their noise showed no sign of abating, and further groups of Flamingos were in the sky, the time had come for action.

"Look, Signora," said Davina in Italian to the nearest *mamma,* "how beautiful those birds are!"

The Italian lady paused for a second in the harangue that she was issuing, and smiled at us – with delight, I am sure, at Davina's mastery of the language. Then she rounded on her young and bellowed the single word: "SILENZIO !!!!"

This had no effect within the Italian party; but the episode did lead to our seeing good concentrations of Flamingos directly above us when we moved a few hundred yards away.

I have taken some clear action photographs from that track on summer evenings (*49 and 53*) – the latter just before take-off: Flamingos require a long run-up, rather like swans. However, to obtain my favourite close-up shots of a pair of birds flying low in perfect light, I spent a scorching afternoon semi-concealed on a spit of land between two lagoons near the Gacholle lighthouse, about a mile to the west of Fangassier, having noticed a few Flamingos moving between the two. There was one particular flight path that would provide the optimal image; after various errors by me and near misses by the birds, two of them eventually took the ideal route (*54*).

The Etang du Fangassier has provided us with our most vivid memories of the Camargue, as epitomised by space, sun, sea, distant hills – and Flamingos. It is a truly idyllic spot. Flamingos are not by any

53: Momentum for take-off: Greater Flamingo, Etang du Fangassier, 1998

54. Elegance: Greater Flamingos, near Gacholle Lighthouse, Camargue, 1997

means the only birds on view. Plovers and Sandpipers feed along the shore: the oddly-named Kentish Plover and the Little Ringed Plover, for example, and the Little Stint. By one of the sluices connecting two lagoons, one regularly sees one or two Little Terns hovering and then diving for small fish.

The area retains a capacity to surprise. One evening, some cyclists appeared on the dry, bumpy track as we awaited the main fly-past. They were evidently heading for the *Digue à la Mer*, and thence to Les Saintes Maries. For all their highly professional attire and equipment, they looked absolutely exhausted. One of them wobbled to a halt beside us and croaked, in otherwise reasonable English, a desperate request for a drop of water. We had some, but not much; the situation evoked old desert movies. When he had imbibed sufficiently for conversation to resume, it emerged that he was German; we are clueless in that language, but we established agreement that the Camargue was an enchanting area.

Davina is not often effusive, but she is thrilled by every visit to the Etang du Fangassier.

"I really think," she enthused, "that this must be the most wonderful sight in the whole world!"

Our new friend paused in the act of draining our water bottle, and carefully surveyed the scene. Then, as he gulped down the final drops, it was clear that there was simultaneously welling up inside him some rejoinder to Davina's euphoria.

"Perhepps," he said gravely, "perhepps not in der *whole* verld."

This good man pedalled solemnly off, bidding us a grateful if slightly baffled farewell. Shamefully, we then collapsed into adolescent giggles. Overhead, some Flamingos seemed to be joining in as they intensified their strange goose-like honking.

55. *Reflection in the Camargue: Black-winged Stilt* (Himantopus himantopus), *La Capellière, Camargue, 2000*

THE CAMARGUE: FURTHER REFLECTIONS, AND THE JEWEL

11

Our holidays in the Camargue are not dedicated solely to the pursuit of birds. One remains gloriously aware that it is a part of France, and for countless reasons it is all the more specially enjoyable for that. Though not uncritical worshippers of all things French, we are intensely attached to France. Our second home, a *mas* on the Mediterranean coast of the Var, approximately half way between Nice and Marseilles, is a source of much pleasure; and we experience a feel-good factor virtually anywhere in the *hexagone*.

We fell for the Department of the Var as long ago as 1968, when we were guests at a house owned by the Eliot family at Cavalaire. This paradise of a place, called Bon Porteau, was our main holiday destination in each subsequent year until 1981, when we were on our posting in Oslo. Much as we loved Norway, we decided that it was a good time to secure a foothold in southern Europe. The south-west coast of the St Tropez peninsula – which is greener and wilder than the rest – was where we sought and found the ideal spot, only ten miles from our previous haunt.

Meanwhile, from 1972 to 1976 I had been First Secretary for Press and Information at our Embassy in Paris, with responsibility for briefing the Paris media, and the British press corps there. It was a challenging time to have this job, which I had longed to get. Britain had just joined the European Community (as it then was). The close relations between President Pompidou and Edward Heath were followed by acrimony over Harold Wilson's "re-negotiation" of the terms of our membership. The French complained that Britain's commitment to Europe was half-hearted, and that we constituted a Trojan Horse for the USA – *plus ça change*. For many commentators in Paris, the cancellation of the (then) Channel Tunnel project in 1975 was further proof of our irredeemable insularity. By the end of our time in Paris, we were trying to reassure these same scribes that Britain's low productivity, bad industrial relations and weak currency were not signs of irreversible economic decline.

Fielding questions on these issues, with help from experts in the appropriate section of the Embassy, was only one part of the job. Each morning, the Press Section was in action very early to scour all the French and British newspapers of the day and assemble a collection of relevant reports and comment, including any fruits of our briefing. We circulated copies of this production before the Ambassador's morning meeting, where it was often the subject of lively gamesmanship around the table.

We also publicised the visits of senior British personalities in many fields, arranging press conferences as necessary. We had to turn our hand to just about anything. At the sublime end of the scale were the glorious experience of a winning day at Chantilly Races with HM The Queen, and a concert by Yehudi Menuhin at Versailles. The reverse came with finding ourselves in the front line for probing from the Red-tops of both capitals after the first in the dreaded series of "Nights of Shame" perpetrated by English soccer fans on the continental mainland. This was the infamous occasion when supporters of Leeds United took apart their end of the Parc des Princes and severely damaged other Parisian properties. There was admittedly some diabolical refereeing in the European Cup Final of 1975, won by Bayern Munich; but many of the Leeds fans were in no condition to assess borderline decisions, having spent the day consuming heavy quantities of alcohol in baking sunshine. The next day, a contact in the French Radio Corporation told me that Jacques Chirac, then Prime Minister of France, would be commenting on the vandalism on the lunch-time news bulletin; would our Ambassador care to say something first? Edward Tomkins gave a masterly interview, which did much to defuse the situation.

I do not say this with arrogance, but there was a perception – which has persisted – that we were in Paris during a *belle époque* for the Embassy. The Ambassador when we arrived was Sir Christopher (later Lord) Soames, the Tory politician and son-in-law of Winston Churchill. In an inspired move, the Labour Government had charged him and his wife Mary with demonstrating to the French that Britain was not only serious in seeking to join the EEC, but also a nation of such stature and style that our continued exclusion would be a loss for both the Community and France. This set the tone and momentum for the Paris Embassy for almost a decade.

We were only on the staff for the Soames' last few months, but we caught the essential flavour, and then enjoyed to the full the enlightened regimes of their successors, Edward and Gill Tomkins and Nicko and

Mary Henderson. A constant sage and catalyst was the Ambassadors' Deputy throughout our entire time, Christopher Ewart-Biggs. He and his wife Jane committed themselves absolutely to getting to the heart of the mindset and genius of the French, in and out of the office. Among many other dividends, this greatly helped to bring the best out of the rest of us. Speaking for myself, it was not as if absolutely everybody there was an exceptionally gifted operator; it was more a matter of the right *conjoncture* producing optimal chemistry among us.

That said, a number of our colleagues in Paris in the 1970s went on to stardom in and out of the Diplomatic Service: Mike Aaronson, Robert Alston, Ronald Arculus, Nicholas Bayne, David Colvin, Timothy Daunt, Howard Davies, Patrick Fairweather, Adrian Fortescue, Anthony Goodenough, Nicky Gordon Lennox, Bill Harding, John Leahy, Humphrey Maud, David Miers, Warwick Morris, Robin Renwick, Ivor Roberts, Nick Spreckley, Derek Thomas, George Walden and Stephen Wall, to name two full XIs off the top of my head (and it would be easy to list others).

The British media were strongly represented in Paris at this time; the period was also a formative one for their French counterparts, seeing the birth of a new morning daily – *Le Quotidien de Paris* – and the television channels *Antenne 2* and FR3. It was a joy to get in at ground-floor level in relations with their editors, journalists and newscasters. I also used to compare notes with the kindred spirit who, early each morning, broadcast on French radio a summary of the main themes in the day's newspapers: this charming person, Patrick Poivre d'Arvor, has since become the top news presenter on French television.

The work was too hectic to permit much reflection and analysis at the time, but I did leave Paris with a greater understanding than I had anticipated of what makes the French tick. Some argue that it can be misleading to assess a country on the basis of experience in its capital alone; they have a point. I had two periods of intensive exposure to regional France, with six weeks of language training in Besançon immediately before starting the job in Paris, to build on a summer spent with a Parisian family on holiday in Brittany, while I was still at Cambridge. These spells were essential preparation for life in Paris. Overall, I believe that the experience of living and working at high speed alongside Parisians for three and a half years left me better qualified to enjoy other, less frenetic parts of France, such as the Camargue; but immersion in provincial France continues to enhance my appreciation of the nation as a whole.

Many have sought, with varying success, to identify the particular qualities of the magnetism of France which can exert such a powerful force on Britons. For some, they are found at intellectual levels – and mainly through contrasts between the French and ourselves. Many French people are Catholic, Cartesian and jesuitical; and they treat the arts as so much more central to life than we do. France also has a more elementary fascination, which can easily spill over into antagonism. It derives from simple geographical factors: besides the Irish (with whom our relations are also complex), the French are our only immediate neighbours – whereas for their part they share frontiers with the major civilisations of Italy, Spain and Germany. So it is small wonder that, for many Britons, perceptions of 'abroad' have traditionally begun at Calais, and contacts with the French have epitomised the hazards of dealing with 'foreigners'.

Personally, I revel in the beauty of the spacious landscapes of France; and I admire the flair of the French people in their pursuit and appreciation of all manner of pleasures, both serious and frivolous. Above all, I enjoy the gusto that they bring to conversations about virtually anything. Whether one is talking with a journalist on the telephone or in a Paris bistro, or to shopkeepers on one's morning rounds in the Var or the Camargue, wit, wisdom, information and challenge all abound. My French interlocutors invariably run rings round me, of course; but I generally come away feeling more cheerful as a result, as well as mentally stimulated.

How the French feel about Britain and the British is even harder to analyse, especially since our performances in and around the EU, NATO and the UN have compounded their innate wariness of us. There are suspicions that some of our insular, unsophisticated attitudes may conceal a devilish cunning. They still make jokes about such hoary stereotypes as our allegedly poor cuisine and our perceived obsession with lavatorial plumbing. Many sincerely admire our monarchy, and envy us for it. The caricature of British reserve may, for some

Frenchmen, still include wisdom and prudence. But the majority are probably now less inclined than before to believe in the proverbial *sang-froid anglais*: our football hooligans and binge drinkers hardly suggest a nation strong on self-control. French people brought up on concepts of British puritanism must feel perplexed, at the very least, if they ever read our mass circulation tabloid newspapers. At the same time they have to stomach the fact that, partly because the Pilgrim Fathers founded the more successful American colonies, English language and culture – however loosely defined – have in many areas supplanted those of the French, which had come so close to global dominance before this eclipse.

*　　*　　*

When friends seek advice about the Camargue, my responses have become increasingly hesitant. Initially, I used to reply with unreserved enthusiasm, and recommend exactly the pattern of our own visits; but it became clear that, for some, this was misleading.

"We did as you suggested, but we have seen more in Norfolk, Palmer!" one dear couple remarked. One could only agree on the excellence of Blakeney and other East Anglian birding venues, and resolve to be more careful; but, as my addiction to the Camargue deepens each year, reticence in conversation about it does not come easily.

Once again, contradictions abound. The Camargue as a whole teems with life; but this does not appear to order in ceaseless displays. Many of the open spaces are just that, and can seem dispiriting in their emptiness of bird life, especially for people in a hurry, or searching in the heat of the day, or when the summer migrants are absent.

Nor is there ubiquitous local expertise to guide the visitor. Enquiries in Les Saintes Maries-de-la-Mer are generally met with pressing encouragement to visit the *Parc Ornithologique*, just to the north of the town. This family enterprise is run efficiently and quite humanely, but the sight of birds in cages – however spacious – tends to depress me. The spirits rise briefly when one sees that, each year, at least one wild pair of White Storks build their enormous nests on top of the enclosure

56. *Catching the eye: Little Egret* (Egretta garzetta), *Les Saintes Maries-de-la-Mer, 2004*

57. The Egret has Landed: Little Egret, La Capellière, Camargue, 1997

58. Treat 'em rough: Little Egrets, Les Saintes Maries-de-la-Mer, 2003

containing their captive brethren – but I then feel even more sorry for the latter. More worthwhile, and spontaneous, is the Reserve at La Capellière, at the eastern end of the Etang de Vaccarès, where a well-kept trail leads to half a dozen hides.

Overall – however complacent this may sound – I believe that it is best to rely on one's own experience and resources. Each visit to the Camargue brings a major surprise or two but, essentially, familiarity and habit hold the key – just as they do for the birds themselves.

Especially in the spring and early summer, there is plenty to see at random as one sets about establishing and checking a pattern of locations favoured by particular species. Together with feeding Flamingos, herons and egrets provide the most frequent casual sightings. The Grey Heron, such a pest to fishermen in Britain, is not persecuted in the Camargue; many live there all year round, with migrants adding to its numbers each winter. I find it a relief not to have to regard this graceful bird, with its hypnotically slow and rhythmic wing-beat, as "the enemy."

The majority of the other species in this group are predominantly summer visitors. A substantial core of Little Egrets remains for the winter; when the summer migrants have joined them, these fine birds become a really frequent sight, feeding in canals or lagoons. As photographic targets, I have found them tantalising: it is difficult to find a balance of light, background and speed of film that does justice to their brilliant whiteness. A lucky exception occurred early one morning, when a splendid individual literally caught my eye over the bank of a canal (56). The plumes down his neck indicate the breeding season. I also like "The Egret has Landed" (57), taken from a hide at La Capellière. For all their graceful displays, parts of their mating ritual are very much on the rough side (58).

Happily, Little Egrets are spreading northwards. My half-brother Charles Ainsworth took a good photograph of one in a field in Kent in 2003. The Daily Telegraph of 13 September 2004 – remarkably, the very day on which I am writing this paragraph – carried a report that, whereas the Little Egret was virtually unknown in Britain 50 years ago, 965 of them had just been counted in Kent and Essex alone. This total is as welcome in the tendency that it reflects as it is astounding in its precision.

59 & 60. It suits us both: Cattle Egret (Bubulcus ibis)*, Camargue, 2001*

61. *Freeze! Juvenile Night Heron* (Nycticorax nycticorax), *La Capellière, Camargue, 1989*

Also present in the Camargue is the Cattle Egret – though not in such numbers as we saw in Cuba. It has not been nesting in the Camargue for so long. From a distance it can be confused with the Little Egret, but – oddly enough – it is smaller, and its bill and legs are paler. This small heron has worked out, over the millennia, that food can be obtained on land at least as easily as in the water. They work in tandem with cattle or horses, and pounce on the grubs, insects, worms and other forms of life that are disturbed in the ground as their "hosts" pull up vegetation for their own food. Cattle Egrets regularly perch on an animal's back, providing a most pleasing spectacle *(59 and 60)*. Occasionally, while still "on board," they peck at insects troubling a horse or cow, thus living up to their French name of *"Héron garde-boeufs"*; but their main business is at the hooves of their vegetarian feeding companions.

A rarer migrant is the Night Heron, which is also very much less conspicuous than the others. We have twice seen a family group at La Capellière, the smart black, white and grey of the adults contrasting with the speckled, bittern-like colours of the juveniles. One year, the group that we were watching suddenly stopped feeding, and froze like statues. I feared that my loading a new film had alarmed them; we then saw that the threat to them was far more serious, as a Marsh Harrier was circling overhead. This handsome raptor is quite common in the reed beds of the Camargue, combining elegance with menace as it seeks to prey on water-birds. The Night Herons remained motionless until the danger was gone; one of the juveniles thus provided me with an obliging close-up *(60)*.

Altogether more prominent, and one of my particular favourites among aquatic species, is the Black-winged Stilt *(55)*. Their black and white livery and their dramatically long, bright pink legs make them an entrancing spectacle as they feed, wading in shallow marshes. Their nesting habits are gregarious, and the courage and co-ordination of their defences exemplary: there is many an ear-splitting sortie as three or four Stilts join in fearless attacks on Marsh Harriers and other potential predators.

One year, I set myself the goal of capturing a Stilt with its mirror image. The requirements appeared to be simple enough: find a Stilt in open water, and establish sun, camera and bird in a straight line. Although the task proved more complex than I had anticipated, I

62. Reflections: Black-winged Stilts (Himantopus himantopus), *Camargue, 2001*

63. *Further reflections: Black-winged Stilts* (Himantopus himantopus)*, Camargue, 2004*

64. *On patrol: Avocet* (Recurvirostra avosetta), *Etang des Launes, Camargue, 2002*

65. Resting: Avocet (Recurvirostra avosetta), *Etang des Launes, Camargue, 2002*

66. Amorous Avocets, Camargue, 2005

eventually achieved some quite satisfactory results – females with the paler crown *(62 and 63)* and the dark-crowned male *(55)*.

Avocets are closely related to Black-winged Stilts, but much less common in the Camargue. Their bodies are slightly larger, but their pale blue legs – though delightfully elegant – are shorter. Their most distinctive feature of all is their upturned bill – familiar to many in Britain in the emblem of the RSPB. Avocets have a special appeal for British birders because, by the middle of the last century, they had almost disappeared from our shores; they have re-established themselves successfully in recent decades, and I have seen several in East Anglia and on the south coast.

In the Camargue, Avocets follow their preference for salt or brackish water. Once I have discovered a nesting colony, I reckon that there there is a reasonable – but not guaranteed – prospect of finding them in the same spot the following year. It was on the basis of this elementary tactic that, in May 2002, we noticed an Avocet in flight, regularly circling some reeds on a small island in the Etang des Launes, to the west of Les Saintes Maries-de-la-Mer. It was just possible, from the shore, to get under his flight path – but would he maintain it? I could scarcely believe my luck as the Avocet duly obliged with a relatively serene fly-past *(64)*. I have also tried to obtain a "mirror" photograph of an Avocet, comparable to those of the Stilt: the results so far have not been perfect, partly because the waters that they frequent are generally less clear and open. But it is still possible to appreciate this fine-looking bird *(65)*. In May 2005 I came upon a pair of Avocets that were feeling too deeply amorous to be concerned about my presence*(66)*.

On land, my main ambition in the Camargue was for a long time a close-up photograph of a European Bee-eater against a background of blue sky – the objective that had eluded me in and around Rome. I searched all over the region for a nesting colony that might provide such an opportunity. Year after year, the results were sub-optimal, though not totally unrewarding: once, as we waited in the hope of a pair of Bee-eaters showing a perfect profile, they were joined by an inquisitive juvenile Hoopoe *(67)*.

Finally, alongside a stream just to the north of Les Saintes Maries-de-la-Mer, we saw three pairs of Bee-eaters hunting dragonflies from

67. *What are these?* Juvenile Hoopoe (Upupa epops) *joins European Bee-eaters* (Merops apiaster), *Camargue, 2000*

68. Holy Grail: European Bee-eater silhouetted, 2001

69. Ready to swoop for dragonflies: European Bee-eaters perched above a stream in the Camargue, 2001

perches just above head height – with nothing but sky behind them. But it was evening, and the light was impossible for photography. I could only set the trusty alarm and creep back first thing in the morning. The day dawned brilliantly fine. The stealth of the approach may not have been as nimble as in the days of the woodpeckers in Cuba, but the excitement was every bit as great. The result *(68)* was a Holy Grail achieved – and the cover for this book. In no other year have we seen Bee-eaters in that particular spot; the insect life above that stream has never been the same. Nor have I since come close to holding in my viewfinder a close image of a Bee-eater silhouetted against the sky. Good fortune was with me that day.

The same outing also provided a nice shot of a pair of Bee-eaters perched at a slightly lower level *(69)*. One can see why Georges Vlassis, in his charming book devoted (in all senses) to *Oiseaux en Camargue*, describes the Bee-eater as the *"véritable joyau"* among them – it certainly is a jewel, and has joined the woodpeckers as my favourite species among land birds. With these, and the Hoopoe in Rome, I felt that I had adequate pictures of two of the four Holy Grail birds that appear together under the label "Order Coraciiformes". (The sub-units within each Order of birds are, in descending rank, the family, the genus and the species. In Europe, the relevant families are bee-eaters, hoopoes, rollers and our small kingfishers. Elsewhere, other families within the Coraciiformes are constituted by larger kingfishers, motmots and todies – we saw examples of all these at various times in Central America and the Caribbean).

My remaining targets, therefore, were the European Roller and the Kingfisher. The latter is the only bird in the group that is a permanent resident in our home latitudes, as opposed to a summer visitor from Africa. I have seen them fleetingly in the Camargue, but my most promising plan to capture an image of one is in the grounds of the Old Rectory at Little Bardfield in Essex, the home of Hugh and Juliet Garmoyle, my son-in-law and daughter – she has already taken a very attractive shot of one. The Roller, on the other hand, only appears very rarely in Britain; the one realistic hope of seeing it has been in the Camargue, and over a full decade we looked out for them in vain there, too.

70. *Beautiful bird, shame about the wire: European Roller* (Coracias garrulus), *Vallée des Baux, 2004*

71. *The Roller's fine wingspan*

72. *Showing his other side, Vallée des Baux, 2005*

It was through the kindness of Rod's father-in-law Drewe Lacey and his friend Peter Waghorn in 2004 that we learned that a promising location for Rollers was a precise spot on the northern fringe of the Camargue, in the Vallée des Baux. We enjoyed the help and hospitality there of the *A Rocha* Community: this is a Christian fraternity dedicated also to the study and protection of wildlife. One of their experts generously included us in a long and memorable walk along an escarpment protruding into the Vallée des Baux, looking down on marshes and farmland. There, we saw our first Rollers – from above. There were two pairs; as part of their mating display, the males were performing spectacular dives, whirling and looping as they plunged, their brilliant blue wing patches glinting. The urge to get closer to one of these many-hued acrobats became ever stronger.

Pursuit of the Roller for photographic purposes proved a more prosaic business, though we needed a full day to get close to one without disturbing it. In the early stages of staking out their territories, and as an aid to their hunting for lizards and frogs, the birds tend to perch on telegraph posts and wires. So there is good access to them by road, and one can get much closer to them in a car than by approaching on foot. It is sometimes difficult to get a good angle on a bird from inside a vehicle, however; the trick in this instance was to emerge surreptitiously and remain concealed behind the car. I obtained a good, clear shot *(70)* with the camera resting on the roof of our Audi. I was wondering how severely the thick black wire would detract from the shimmering colours of the Roller when the bird prepared himself for take-off . . . I took a picture as he left, but was uncertain as to whether I had caught him in his entirety, and clear of the wire. Luck was with me again *(71)*. I attributed it to the magic of the Camargue. Visiting the same valley in May 2005, I was once more fortunate with a shot of this Roller in flight*(72)*.

73. *Unexpected bonus: Scarlet Macaw (Ara macao), Puerto Jiménez, Costa Rica, 2003*

12

PURSUIT OF THE EXOTIC IN COSTA RICA

In our journey to spend twelve days in Costa Rica in the spring of 2003, we departed from the pattern of our working lifetime. For 35 years, we had travelled to live in places where the FCO had been good enough to send us, and enjoyed whatever birds we came across in and around those foreign capitals. By contrast, we were heading for San José specifically to search for birds – and over 800 species are to be found in Costa Rica.

There was however a welcome degree of Diplomatic Service continuity in our trip, for we were invited to Costa Rica by the British Ambassador there, Georgina Butler. This delightful lady had the misfortune to be my subordinate when she arrived as a new entrant to the Service to join the Southern European Department of the FCO in 1968. As Head of Mission in San José, Georgina embarked on a particularly happy phase of her life: not only the proverbial Place of Her Own, but also marriage to Robert Kelly, whom we were delighted to meet out there. San José has an idyllic climate, lying at over 4,000 feet in the broad Central Valley, surrounded by magnificent green mountains.

Costa Rica is so named because of the rumours (erroneous) of vast treasures of gold there, which circulated at the time of its discovery during Columbus's last voyage in 1502. This beautiful little country has since been known for its exports of fine coffee and fruit, especially bananas; for its enlightened social welfare and environmental policies; and – not least – for having no army (it was abolished in 1949). Latterly, tourism has taken over from the agricultural produce as Costa Rica's principal industry. Happily, much of the emphasis has remained on "ecotourism," with medium-sized and small hotels and ranches offering visitors access to the country's wonderful variety of habitats for birds and other wildlife. This approach is compatible with the Costa Rican authorities' efforts to resist the distressing global trends whereby the rainforest, and biodiversity more generally, are under increasing threat.

With the help of advice from Georgina herself and from one of her predecessors, Willie Marsden, a friend of mine since Winchester days, we decided to divide our time between the Caribbean and Pacific "slopes" of Costa Rica. Many of the country's birds are to be found only on one of these; and a good proportion of them are very much more specialised than that in their requirements for their habitat. We made our

74. *Delicately pretty: Blue and Grey Tanager* (Thraupis episcopus)*, San José, Costa Rica, 2003*

reservations by internet from Britain; on the Caribbean side, we chose an inland location, and, to the west, a ranch beside the Pacific Ocean. Both promised good viewing of species of birds that we had never seen before: even in Cuba and Mexico, both relatively close to Costa Rica, there had been (apart from aquatic birds) only a handful of woodpeckers, flycatchers and kingbirds that were also to be seen on this trip. Otherwise, Costa Rica's treasures would be new to us.

Before setting out from the capital, we enjoyed the splendour of Georgina's garden – and the birds there. A prominent visitor was the Blue and Grey Tanager *(74)*. We saw these delicately pretty birds in all the other parts of Costa Rica that we visited. From the breakfast table on Georgina's terrace, we could watch several species of hummingbird darting among the flowers: I managed to catch a male Rufous-tailed Hummingbird having his own breakfast *(75)*. Hummingbirds only occur in the New World. Although they also feed on insects, their foraging for nectar provides the best views of their iridescent colours and their spectacular manner of flight, in which they use their unique rotation of the entire wing at the shoulder joint. This enables them radically to change the angle of their wingbeat and to hover in place and fly backwards as they feed from flowers. Hummingbirds are also notable for their pugnacity: they are most aggressive at their feeding territories.

Our destination to the east of San José was Rancho Naturalista, a family-run concern near the town of Turrialba. The guidebooks describe the latter as a pleasant centre for agriculture and tourism. Regrettably, our memories of it are wholly without affection, for it was there that we were robbed of my main camera, a Nikon F100. The thieves' technique was, we later learned, classic in those parts, with hired cars – readily identifiable from their number plates – a regular target. An accomplice must have pierced one of our tyres in a traffic jam as we entered the town. In half a mile or so we were running on the rim, and a group of seemingly helpful young men emerged from the car behind us to offer help in changing the wheel, and getting the punctured tyre to a service station for repair. This chatty squad "happened" to have connections there, and the numbers around our car, and the volume of conversation, increased as the work progressed.

As we moved off, our rescuers waved us on our way with beaming

75. *Nectar: Rufous-tailed Hummingbird (male)* (Amazilia tzacatl), *San José, Costa Rica 2003*

76. Easy to hover, and reverse: Rufous-tailed Hummingbird (female), Tuis, Costa Rica, 2003

smiles; nothing seemed amiss, and their amiable attitude seemed consistent with the reputation of *ticos,* as Costa Ricans are known, for being charming and welcoming; generally, this is well deserved. It was only when we unloaded the car on arrival at the ranch that we found that the F100 had disappeared. The villains had distracted us for long enough to grab it. We felt very foolish, and furious; but at least the reserve Nikon, an F80, and the zoom lens were still with us.

A symbolically traumatic moment coincided with our frantic search for the missing camera. Davina paused for breath in our futile thrashing around among our baggage; as she looked over the balcony, she pointed out a medium-sized snake advancing towards the terrace of our building. She has a phobia of all snakes, and I sought to reassure her that, according to the guidebook, most of those in Costa Rica were harmless. Shortly afterwards, however, the hotel staff warned us, with illustrations, of the occasional presence in the area of the dreaded *fer-de-lance* – described in the same guidebook as "one of the world's deadliest snakes". There was not the slightest doubt from the markings, which were indeed a series of spear-heads, that this sinister reptile was what we had just seen.

Early the next morning, my humour was partially restored when a female Rufous-tailed Hummingbird hovered outside the balcony of our room for long enough for me to attempt a photograph of it. One of the many merits of the F100 is the superlative speed of its focussing and all its other operations, and I feared that its loss might prove critical; but the stand-in machine appeared to meet the demands of this situation – and so, happily, it proved *(76).*

We then set off in a group of a dozen or so, mainly tourists from the USA with extensive ornithological knowledge, and correspondingly formidable attire and equipment. They were without exception charming, generous and tolerant companions. We were in the care of an American guide, Steve. He was impressive: young, entertaining and above all brilliantly intuitive in his assessments of the habits and reactions of the birds of the region. It was a privilege to acquire knowledge from him. Following his patient guidance, we saw some remarkable inhabitants of the understory of the forest: the Immaculate Antbird and the Spotted Antbird. These are certainly insect eaters, but

77. Surveying the valley: Montezuma Oropendola (Psarocolius montezuma)*, Tuis, Costa Rica, 2003*

78. Related to the Bee-eaters: Broad-billed Motmot (Electron platyrhynchum)*, Tuis, Costa Rica, 2003*

they acquire their name from accompanying armies of ants and foraging with them, seizing spiders and other insects that the column dislodges, as opposed to devouring the ants themselves. Antbirds' colouring provides them with camouflage on the floor of the forest, as one would expect; but several species also have dramatic white streaks and bars, and blue patches around their heads.

I can become uneasy in guided groups, especially if – as in this instance – I am the only person trying to take photographs of the birds that are observed: this carries the risk of repeatedly keeping the others waiting, and consequently makes me feel under pressure. It is often better to settle for listening carefully to the expert, marking down likely subjects, and returning alone later – if time permits. But I was able, on our excursions with Steve, to get reasonable shots of a Montezuma Oropendola *(77)*, and a Broad-billed Motmot *(78)*. Having heard the latter's hooting call, Steve found the bird for us in a patch of particularly dark rainforest, where I was glad of the flash that is built in to the Nikon F80: the camera that had started the trip as the reserve was rising magnificently to this and most other challenges. The Motmot's racquet-tipped tail, and its position in the same order of birds as the Bee-eaters, made it a very exciting trophy. The Oropendola was much easier to find, preferring open country, and weaving wonderful purse-like nests that dangle from isolated trees.

When Davina and I retraced our steps that afternoon, we made more leisurely progress along a humid valley frequented by hummingbirds. I was very keen to photograph the White-necked Jacobin, a most attractive species – *(79)* shows the male and *(80)* the female. Whereas the Rufous-tailed and several other hummingbirds can be seen all year round in Costa Rica, the Jacobin disappears from both sides of the country between September and December – and nobody has yet been able to determine where they all go to. Another remarkable hummingbird seen by streams around the ranch was the Snowcap: the male is deep purple, with a brilliant white crown. They are almost as tiny as the Bee Hummingbirds we had seen in Cuba; locals in Costa Rica told us that the Snowcap is able to hold its own among the many larger species because several of the latter are alarmed by the colour white. Larger hummingbirds that we saw included the

79 & 80. In autumn, they disappear: White-necked Jacobin (male and female) (Florisuga mellivora), *Tuis, Costa Rica, 2003*

Green-breasted Mango; the Brown Violet-ear; and the Crowned Woodnymph.

Steve had pointed out to us a Collared Aracari – a sort of Toucan – in flight, and told me the approximate area where we should be able to see them feeding or at rest. Davina and I took a morning off from the group to try to track them down. On our way, we saw Scarlet-rumped Tanagers – the male precisely fits the description – and two species of Tityra, smart-looking grey and black birds, not unlike flycatchers. The Masked Tityra is, we were told, much more common than the Black-crowned; but they sometimes inhabit the same tree, and this is what we saw. We then contemplated the hillside of relatively open woodland that Steve had recommended. There was no movement. I scanned the vegetation through the zoom lens; Davina had binoculars.

"Is that a strange leaf sticking out from that tree?" I asked. Her reply was exactly what I longed to hear.

"No – it's a beak!"

We had found an Aracari's nest – in what had initially been a woodpecker's hole. The rest of the morning was riveting. For a while, the huge, subtly shaded bill remained motionless. It then emerged to the point where we could also see the bird's bright yellow eye and the front of its underparts *(81)*. I waited, poised to release the shutter as he took off – and did so. Sadly, it was here that the speed of the stolen F100 really was badly missed, for the resultant shot shows only the scarlet rump of the Aracari disappearing into the undergrowth.

I kept the camera locked on the same spot; we saw several Aracaris come and go, and read later that as many as five adults may attend a nest – thus outperforming even the European Bee-eater in familial diligence and co-operation. I then moved a short distance away for the main objective, which remained an Aracari perching in the open; one eventually obliged *(82)*, against the background of the steep valley.

The experience with the Aracaris offset my disappointment at failing to get close to any of the Keel-billed Toucans that we saw on the Caribbean side of Costa Rica. Although no photographs of them were feasible, we saw them well enough to appreciate why this larger species is also – and more appropriately – called the Rainbow-billed Toucan, and how it has become such a frequent choice for tourist literature and postcards.

81. Not just a leaf: Collared Aracari (Pterroglossus torquatus), *Tuis, Costa Rica, 2003*

82. The whole bird: Collared Aracari, Tuis, Costa Rica, 2003

Any birdwatching venture is of course greatly enhanced for me by the presence of woodpeckers. There are some 16 species in Costa Rica. The individual providing me with the best pose on the Caribbean side of the country was a male Hoffmann's Woodpecker *(83)*. This handsome bird, with its dramatic golden-yellow nape, is common in many areas of Costa Rica (it is slightly smaller than our Great Spotted Woodpecker).

We returned to San José with a heap of laundry for Georgina's charming Residence staff, and an embarrassed tale to tell to the Police. We then set off in a small aircraft for the Pacific coast. I had been delighted by the range of birds that we had already seen, but several priority targets remained, notably the good selection of trogons – a dozen species – that inhabit Costa Rica. We had however abandoned any hope of seeing in the wild on this visit that ultimate trophy for birders in Costa Rica, the Resplendent Quetzal (itself a member of the trogon family). The male is a glittering green bird, with streaming tail feathers two feet long. Its preferred habitats are in forested mountains, at levels which pressures of time prevented us visiting. We saw one in captivity outside San José; it looked understandably sorry for itself.

The Scarlet Macaw, on the other hand, remained a gleam in my eye – though not a very confident one. I had read that, in 1900, these magnificent great birds were abundant on both the Caribbean and Pacific sides of the country. Now, there were few significant populations, and the best chance of seeing them would be in the Pacific lowlands, especially the Osa Peninsula. We were due to change aircraft at Puerto Jiménez, the only settlement of any size on that Peninsula; but there would be no time to spare between our arrival there and our departure in an even smaller aircraft to Tiskita Jungle Lodge – away from the Osa Peninsula. Moreover, we had read that Scarlet Macaws spent most of their time in the canopy of the rainforest, so a fleeting glimpse was the most that one could sensibly anticipate. I feared that the guidebook was raising false hopes when stating that Puerto Jiménez was still sufficiently remote to enable visitors to see parrots and macaws flying around. And yet . . .

As we pulled up on the airstrip cut out of the forest outside Puerto Jiménez, two things struck me. Ours was the only aircraft there; and two large, bright red birds were visible in a tree a short distance from the sheds that constituted the terminal buildings. I attached the zoom lens and headed straight for that tree, abandoning wife, baggage and contingency travel plans. For, miraculously, it was a pair of Scarlet Macaws; and I shot off a full roll of film before being called to order by the genial authorities. They informed us that the Air Taxi to Tiskita would not fly that day, and that we would have to go there by road from Golfito, across the bay from Puerto Jiménez, where our San José aircraft could drop us off if we hurried.

"But . . . *las Lapas Rojas* . . ." I pleaded. It was in vain: further delay would compel us to travel a further 50 miles by road round the bay to Golfito, before setting off on the drive of similar distance (but on far worse roads) to Tiskita. One could only hope that the delicious fluke that had brought me face to face with a pair of Scarlet Macaws would somehow recur on our homeward journey – but that seemed a very long shot, and the birds in my pictures were visible only down to their breasts.

Tiskita Jungle Lodge is a heavenly place. It is remote, in the extreme south-western corner of Costa Rica, only ten miles from the frontier with Panama. The accommodation is comfortable, in rustic but well-appointed cabins spread generous distances apart. From the balcony surrounding our abode, we could look down to the Pacific breakers on the beach, with flotillas of Brown Pelicans beyond, and also up to the rainforest. Wildlife was all around. Each morning, parties of Capuchin and Spider Monkeys descended on foraging expeditions, their prehensile tails and long limbs enabling them to perform phenomenal acrobatics as they swung past us.

Even our bathroom was open to the rainforest: while brushing my teeth one morning, I saw a pair of Golden-naped Woodpeckers – darker all over than Hoffmann's, and equally small. These enchanting little birds are found only in this part of Costa Rica and the adjoining region of Panama. My attempt to photograph them as I slithered around the bathroom was scrambled in all senses. The other species in this family that we saw at Tiskita were the Red-crowned Woodpecker – reminiscent of the Golden-fronted that we had seen in Mexico, but smaller – and the large, splendid Lineated Woodpecker, also previously seen in the Yucatán.

Our guide on our walks through the forest and orchards of Tiskita was the proprietor of the Lodge himself, Peter Aspinall, a fascinating person.

83. *Further variations: Hoffmann's Woodpecker*
(Melanerpes hoffmannii), *Tuis, Costa Rica, 2003*

84. *Star in the canopy of the rainforest: Baird's Trogon (male)* (Trogon bairdii), *Tiskita Lodge, Costa Rica, 2003*

Part American, part Costa Rican, with a charming Costa Rican wife, Peter approaches all aspects of his domain with total commitment and contagious enthusiasm. He has ambitious plans to market the many varieties of tropical fruit in his orchards. Meanwhile he revels in helping visitors to Tiskita to understand something of the incredibly abundant wildlife there. On our walks in the rainforest, his interpretation of every sound – whether of an animal, a bird or an insect – was a revelation. Throughout our visit, he enabled us to see numerous forms of life which, left to ourselves, we should never have noticed. As with Steve on the Caribbean slope, this applied particularly to ground-dwelling birds. The Riverside Wren, for example, lives in dense undergrowth but, once Peter had pointed it out, one could admire its smart black and white barred chest. He also drew our attention to Woodcreepers – the Streaked-headed and the Barred – as they moved up the trunks of trees; though they are several times the size of our European Treecreeper, they are well camouflaged, and I could easily have missed them.

Yet there were surprises in the forest even for Peter Aspinall. He had already identified for us the resonant voice of the Howler Monkey, which carries over half a mile or more. It is a larger species than the two that swung through the trees by our cabin, and less frequently seen. As we continued on our walk, we heard more Howlers, apparently together. Peter listened to them carefully, and concluded that one might be injured, or even dead: we should make a detour to investigate. It proved that the Howler Monkeys had indeed gathered – in evident distress – following the death of a large male. Peter was sure that the monkey had simply died of old age; he prepared to bury him, telling us that the group would suffer further if the corpse was devoured by carrion-feeding creatures.

Just as the Howler Monkeys' commotion was reaching its peak, Peter said that he had heard the call of a trogon – it would, he said, be either the Slaty-tailed or Baird's Trogon. We agreed that Davina and I would try to track it down while he completed the last rites of the monkey. We were fortunate, and soon found a pair of Baird's Trogons; I obtained a decent picture of the male (84). Like its Cuban relative, this handsome bird showed a generous degree of calm as I set up the tripod and camera. He was perching quite high up in a dark patch of forest, and the F80's flash was again indispensable. The dark velvety blue of his neck made the red

85. Confident: Broad-winged Hawk (Buteo platypterus), *Tiskita Lodge, Costa Rica, 2003*

86. Noisy squabble: Scarlet Macaws (Ara macao), *Puerto Jiménez, Costa Rica, 2003*

of his breast still more vivid. The photograph gives only a glimpse of the blue-green of his back. Whereas both genders of the Cuban Trogon are identical, the female Baird's Trogon – slightly more shy, and also a very fine-looking bird – showed more delicate, pink and grey markings. The Howler Monkeys' much-lamented loss had led to our gain. From the illustrations that I had seen of all the species of trogons to be found in Costa Rica, the male Baird's was the loveliest (apart from the Resplendent Quetzal), and its range is confined to the Pacific regions of Costa Rica and Panama.

Back out in the open, there were a number of Chestnut-mandibled Toucans at Tiskita: they are even larger than the Keel-bills, and almost as spectacular in their colours. But they were, sadly, equally reluctant to come within photographic range: with great respect to the Aracaris, this was a major disappointment. I was more fortunate with a Broad-winged Hawk *(85)*. This impressive bird is among the many that breed in North America and sensibly migrate in winter to Central and South America.

Other raptors prominently on view at Tiskita were the Laughing Falcon and the Yellow-headed Caracara. Both are handsome birds, predominantly buff and brown in colour – apart from the Laughing Falcon's black mask, resembling that of a cartoon burglar. Larger than either, and even more spectacular, was the American Swallow-tailed Kite. In flight – and it spends more time on the wing than other raptors – it appears mainly white, though its deeply forked tail is darker. I saw one gliding over the Aspinall orchards for a good ten minutes, only rarely flapping its long and graceful wings – and even in swooping for a lizard or insect it required remarkably few wingbeats. I have seen few lovelier birds.

All too soon, the time came for us to take wing ourselves. Peter walked down with us to the grass airstrip between the ranch and the classically palm-fringed beach. As we told him, we would gladly have stayed for a month at Tiskita. We circled in our single-engine plane and turned away from that enchanted domain. As it disappeared, I turned my attention to a moment of truth that was approaching: would the Scarlet Macaws still be around the little airfield at Puerto Jiménez?

As we came in to land, there was no bird life in the tree where they had been before. But, once again, the connecting plane was late, so there

87. Quiet when feeding: Scarlet Macaw, Puerto Jiménez, Costa Rica, 2003

was time to look further afield – and raucous cries in some high trees only a quarter of a mile away revealed that the Macaws were still in the area. I scrambled off and arrived out of breath to watch six of them flying around in restless and, in the case of two birds, quarrelsome style *(86)*. Things became calmer when one pair of Macaws flew away.

I had agreed with Davina that I would look back at her from time to time through my binoculars, and return to the airfield if she indicated that this was necessary. I soon saw her waving vigorously. There was nothing for it; I went panting back to join her.

"So – where's the plane?" I demanded.

"I wasn't calling you for that," she said quietly, "look over there."

The two Scarlet Macaws that had left the high trees were eating almonds from the very same tree where we had seen them before, and their entire forms, all of 33 inches in length, were visible. I marvelled at the other colours – yellow, deep blue and sky blue – that adorned their wings, alongside the brilliant red *(73 and 87)*. The books inform us that, while the voice of the Scarlet Macaw is exceptionally resonant even by parrots' standards, the birds are usually quiet when feeding: these two behaved accordingly. They also seemed unperturbed when I ventured closer to them – perhaps they were tired and hungry after their exertions in the tall trees. Either way, they provided some of the most memorable spectacles of the whole holiday.

There is some nice irony in comparing the macaw episodes with experiences such as those with the Broad-billed Motmot and Baird's Trogon. Both of those exotic trophies were the fruit of long jungle walks, whereas the Scarlet Macaws, for all my pessimism about the likelihood of seeing them at all, seemed if anything to have sought us out. The arrival of our aircraft interrupted further reflection on how this good fortune had compensated further for my failure to get sufficiently close to the two principal toucans.

As we left Puerto Jiménez, our pilot – an experienced, agreeable, no-nonsense type – was instructed to divert to the coastal resort of Quepos to collect two more passengers before proceeding to San José. Before we landed there, we could see heavy storm clouds in the mountains between the Pacific and the capital. The new passengers then kept us waiting for three-quarters of an hour before they deigned to appear at the airfield. There were three of them, not two; and they had a lot of baggage. They were young male Americans: all were surly, ill-mannered and – most worryingly – overweight. The pilot, though anxious to get away and much irritated by the delay, took great care in loading us all in. The clouds had become blacker and more menacing. The euphoria of the encounters with the Scarlet Macaws evaporated swiftly.

It is hard to describe that flight adequately. The words "white" and "knuckle" spring to mind, along with other clichés that are better suppressed. I was seated in the least disagreeable position, alongside our excellent pilot: I could follow his exchanges with the control tower in San José, which included instant rejection of their offer of landing at an alternative airport. I also liked to think that I could sense his steady control of the plane as it was buffeted by thunderous gusts and battered by massive sheets of rain. For Davina, huddled beside the ghastly Americans, there was no such solace: even the immigration officials in New York a couple of days later seemed affable by comparison with those monsters. We were as pleased to get away from them as we were grateful to our pilot – and he was not the only authority to whom we offered heartfelt thanks as we stepped unsteadily from his craft on arrival. The Americans did not address a single word to him. One could only hope that our courteous and expert birding companions on the Caribbean side of Costa Rica were more typical representatives of the USA.

Our last day was spent relaxing with Georgina and Robert in San José. They continued to look after us wonderfully. One of the birds in their garden was the national bird of Costa Rica. This is not, as one might have imagined, one of the many spectacular species resident in that country, but the Clay-coloured Robin. In appearance, the bird is as unremarkable as its name suggests. But it is a character, notable for its fearless mobbing of Brown Jays and other potential predators of its nest and, even more so, for its richly melodious song, which has earned it the name 'Yigüirro' and helped us to depart on a happy note.

88. Bird on head: Grey Wagtail (Motacilla ceneria)*, West Wycombe, 2004*

13

SUNDRY OPPORTUNITIES: BE PREPARED!

With the passing of the years, I have become steadily less well suited – physically and temperamentally – to long journeys, let alone to the nomadic pattern of a diplomat's life. But, despite the onset of sedentary feelings, I have to admit that almost any form of travel carries the bonus of wider possibilities for spotting and observing birds.

Even a mere ten miles from home, during an enthralling day's fishing at West Wycombe, I am easily distracted these days by the swans, Tufted Duck and other birds on the lake and along the river; and I always have my camera with me, as well as binoculars. An amusing opportunity occurred last summer when a Grey Wagtail, a most attractive bird that habitually nests in crevices near the cascade where the River Wye flows from the Dashwoods' lake, perched on a statue above the waterfall *(88)*. I have also had excellent views at West Wycombe of some of the Red Kites that have recently been so successfully reintroduced to the Chilterns. I first became aware of this cheering development when I saw them from the cutting in the M40 at Bledlow Ridge. They have since become regular visitors to Little Missenden.

The most spectacular intrusion by a bird on my efforts to catch trout occurred long ago, in Norway in 1981. I was fishing on a lake some 30 miles outside Oslo. I had noticed a large bird soaring high above, but thought little of it. The trout, which had been quiet in the heat of the afternoon, became active as evening approached: they were rising keenly to insects on the surface. I was keeping as still as I could and concentrating hard on a series of promising rises by one particular fish. Then, only 30 feet from me, there was a sudden flurry and splashing as a powerful black and white form swooped on the surface of the lake. It was the bird that I had seen earlier but forgotten: a magnificent Osprey, over 20 inches in length. Its streamlined dive was deadly in its precision. Its eye, set in a dark band on its white head, glinted as it altered the angle of its long wings and carried away in its talons a trout that had also been moving nearby, which must have weighed at least a pound and a half.

My mind wanders all the more readily from fish to fowl when salmon are the intended prey. I have enjoyed generous hospitality from family and friends in Scotland, and very occasionally even landed fish from the Rivers Deveron, Spey and Helmsdale. But, whereas one is usually aware

89. By the Helmsdale telephone box: Willow Warbler (Phylloscopus trochilus)*, Kildonan, Sutherland, 2000*

of where a trout is lying and how it is behaving, pursuit of salmon is a more random process, in which I tend quite soon to reach my personal limit for maintaining razor-sharp concentration on every inch of water covered by my imperfectly presented fly. Moreover, not only is the scenery glorious on those three rivers, but the bird life is also varied and interesting. Dippers can be seen foraging in the rapids; I shall never forget the juvenile Wrens that hurtled around the bank of the Spey and disappeared like furry brown squash balls into the foliage beside me. Oystercatchers pipe the fisherman along the Helmsdale, in particular.

However meagre the catch, high spirits have prevailed on all the Scottish salmon fishing parties in my experience, particularly when I was with my father on the Spey and, more recently, when my brother-and sister-in-law David and Gillie Keown-Boyd have been present in hilarious Harley-inspired gatherings on the Helmsdale. As a fisherman, David is vastly more expert than I am; but we share an eye and an ear for entertaining nuances on and off the river. One year, we were told that a pair of Willow Warblers was nesting near a telephone box at Kildonan, some way along the river from the beat where we were fishing. It was David's turn to fish at the time, so I hurried off alone to investigate, taking my camera and binoculars.

There was no mistaking the location. Dwellings are sparsely scattered along the strath of the Helmsdale, and telephone boxes are rarer still: this was, in fact, the only one for many miles. (The agreeable remoteness of this part of the far north of Scotland was accentuated by the unavail-ability of any signal on my mobile telephone). I started to look for the little birds about 50 yards from the telephone box. They were hard at work feeding their young; the nest was at ground level, a yard in from the road, and the same distance from the telephone box. I got quite close before they showed any sign of alarm. I then retreated for a moment but, on the reasonable assumption that people – if not all that many – had been using that telephone in recent weeks without putting the warblers off, decided to enter the box.

The birds immediately resumed their activity, only darting away when, in an attempt to get a clearer photograph, I started to open the door of the cabin. I readily settled for pictures taken through the glass *(89)*, while the birds took very little notice of me. I finished the film and returned to

90. *Lovely bird, but I was late with my packing: Little Green Bee-eater* (Merops orientalis), *Muscat, 1989*

91. *Keeping out the cold: American Robin* (Turdus migratorius), *Central Park, New York, 1989*

the river, where the salmon were dormant (or, for all we could tell, absent). David Keown-Boyd and George Sutherland, the excellent ghillie, were happy to accompany me back to the Willow Warblers' nest. When I told them that the birds would be untroubled by observation from inside the box, David and George went straight in – and I could not resist squeezing in with them. We had a brilliant view as the warblers continued to scurry to and fro, bearing insects and other tiny items of nourishment for their brood.

The road running north-west at this point is proudly labelled the A897, but it is no more than a single track (with passing places). Its main users are sheep, at a ratio of several hundred for each vehicle that passes. But it just happened that a couple of Land Rovers came by the telephone box, one in each direction, at the very moment when three eminently recognisable males were crammed inside it. They carried other fishermen on the Helmsdale, and plenty more was heard that week about the weird antics of the Willow Warbler watchers. Locally, George Sutherland may not yet have lived the matter down.

*　　*　　*

The Duke of Kent made regular overseas trips each year when I was his Private Secretary, several of them in His Royal Highness's capacity as Chairman of the British Overseas Trade Board. During the 'Oman With Britain' week in Muscat in 1989, the Duke kindly agreed to my slipping away at 0500 one morning to photograph the Little Green Bee-eater, which is indeed smaller – by three inches – than the European species. I managed to record the charming bird *(90)*, but the outing took longer than I had estimated. Only some smart help with my packing from the Duke's valet, a most affable Sergeant in the Scots Guards, saved me from falling behind the official programme – much to the amusement of our excellent hosts at the Embassy, Robert and Pat Alston.

On our next trip, which was to promote British exports to the USA in Houston and New York, I only indulged in bird photography when safely in the main body of our party. On an early morning walk in Manhattan's Central Park, I paused briefly to snap an American Robin against the icy blue sky *(91)*. A good ten inches long, this smart fellow is almost twice

92. *Huge nest on a housetop: White Stork* (Ciconia ciconia), *Tunisia, 1989*

the size of our own Robin, being a true thrush. The American bird is only a rare vagrant on this side of the Atlantic.

While planning the Duke of Kent's programme in Tunisia in 1990, which he was to carry out as President of the Commonwealth War Graves Commission, I was excited at the prospect of visiting the celebrated Lake Ishkeul. I had seen on television that Flamingos and other species could be seen there in large numbers. I duly set off for some serious reconnaissance with Inspector Reg Reynolds, the Duke's Protection Officer, who had become a very good friend. We drove round the shores of the lake for many miles – and saw only a gull or two. The migratory population had not arrived, and would not do so in time for the Duke's visit: item deleted. At least, I reflected, we had spared the Duke from journeying out to Lake Ishkeul merely to witness a waterside non-event. It would have been as bleak in reality as the desolation twice claimed by Sir Bedivere, when the dying King Arthur bade him throw the sword Excalibur into a different lake – Tennyson's couplet has been with me since prep school:–

"I heard the ripple washing in the reeds,
And the wild water lapping on the crag."

Reg and I also consoled ourselves by taking some photographs of White Storks that had built nests on the roofs of houses in a village on the way back to Tunis *(92)*. On returning to the residence of the Ambassador – my old friend Stephen Day – I had good views of Hoopoes and Little Owls in his superb garden near the ruins of Carthage; these presaged my experiences in Rome a few years later.

When I was in the USA for the Bilderberg Meeting of 1997, I remained true to the maxim of never leaving my camera behind. The conference was at Pine Isle, outside Atlanta, Georgia. I had tempting glimpses of Eastern Bluebirds and Brown Thrashers, but the schedule was very busy and I had time only to stalk and snap a male Northern Cardinal on the golf course adjoining the hotel *(93)*. These magnificent birds – they are large finches, who sing beautifully – have expanded their range in North America, and I sometimes wonder how they would fare if introduced on our side of the Atlantic. They can be quite feisty, and I suspect that they would look after themselves successfully; but our

93. Sounds as good as he looks: Northern Cardinal (Cardinalis cardinalis), *Pine Isle, Georgia, USA, 1997*

resident finches could suffer as the Cardinals set about establishing their niche.

It is easy enough, at home or away, to find one's day enhanced by the sight or sound of birds, and to enjoy it without inconvenience to others. Stopping to take a picture of a bird on an expedition where photography is not the object of the exercise is another matter. But I do not expect ever to be cured of the urge to do so.

94. *Binoculars always to hand: Davina on an official outing in Santiago de Cuba, July 1988. The mountains are the Sierra Maestra, where Fidel Castro's Revolution began in the 1950s*

"Don't look back!" is advice that I hear from time to time. Readers who have persevered this far will be aware that I am not of that persuasion: I do not regard moments spent treasuring memories as time wasted. What I do believe to be fruitless, on the other hand, is indulgence in regretful speculation at what might have been – unless there is a lesson to be drawn from it for some present or future circumstances, and it is generally best to keep such conclusions to oneself.

Few people, perhaps not even the irredeemably smug minority who so appal me, pretend to have had lives of uninterrupted fulfilment and enjoyment. Of course there are negative sides to a diplomatic career, such as frustration, exhaustion and – for those so inclined, like myself – anxiety in abundance. Some may wonder whether I had my share of disappointment: would I, for example, have preferred to end my career at a larger mission than the Embassy to the Holy See?

When we left for Rome in 1991, there was time for two more postings, and I did not expect the Vatican to be my last job. I had my eye on Oslo: we had thrived in Norway, had many good friends and contacts there, and I had learned the language. After a couple of years in Rome, I was told that someone else had got the top job in Oslo. Some less appealing possibilities were mentioned, and we preferred the alternative of two more years in Rome, followed by retirement at the age of 59 rather than 60.

This solution was in several respects ideal. The Pope's high profile in the Balkans, Northern Ireland and other areas involving British interests meant that my regular dealings with the Vatican entailed work that was both plentiful and absorbing. Our perception of the benefits of living in Rome for four years, as opposed to only two, will be clear enough from previous chapters. Even the timing of our return to Britain proved fortunate: if it had been a few months later, I would have missed the opportunity of working for Lord Carrington on the Bilderberg Meetings from 1996 to 1999.

And yet . . . in 1995, as the moment approached for embarking on the "after-life" as my witty colleague Martin Morland called it, I did feel a bit sad and vulnerable. Stupidly, I made some of my friends aware of these unworthy emotions. Consequently, when I was paying my farewell calls in London, I found that senior figures in the FCO Administration were prepared for me to express some such chagrin. By then, however, I had pulled myself together and could in all sincerity emphasise to them the point already made in the first chapter of this book: that my predominant feelings towards the Diplomatic Service were appreciation and gratitude.

And so they should be. All of my postings in London, where I had at various times worked on southern Europe, NATO, and Latin America, had been exciting, with frequent exposure to Ministers and Parliament. Our overseas appointments – in La Paz, Ottawa, Paris, Oslo, Havana and Rome – made an appetising list. I had ever since my youth longed to get to know people in foreign lands, and to try to understand their motivation, their culture and their view of Britain. It was all a privilege, from the first; moving on to the last, I am not aware of anyone else who has been accredited to both Fidel Castro and to Pope John Paul II, two of the truly larger-than-life figures of our time. Along the way, the FCO provided timely instruction and refreshment by arranging for me to attend sabbatical courses at the Royal College of Defence Studies (in 1978) and the Harvard Centre for International Affairs (in 1985-86). They also showed imagination and flexibility over my secondment to HRH the Duke of Kent from 1988 to 1990.

David Burns, an old friend who retired at around the same time as me (he was Ambassador to Cambodia, and then to Finland) felt strongly that more should be done to retain the bonds and the proverbial *esprit de corps* between former members of the Diplomatic Service. The Office encouraged him to do something about it – and by 1999 the Foreign and Commonwealth Office Association (FCOA) was up and running, with David the Founder Chairman. It now has some 2,000 members. I have supported the FCOA keenly, and have been on its Committee since 2002; we have a first-rate new Chairman in Roger Westbrook.

Only rarely do FCOA fixtures clash with my work at Reading, where I remain on the Finance and General Purposes and other Committees of the Council. Like most Universities, we have plenty to occupy us there as we grapple with financial issues, including the controversial top-up fees, and other politically driven factors such as wider participation. I am also engaged in fund-raising for the University: one of our projects is to relocate the Museum of English Rural Life in a building once inhabited by my biscuit-making ancestors, who were significant benefactors of the University in its early years – if only I could match their philanthropy.

The FCOA's aims include creating occasions for members to meet friends old and new, and the monitoring of retirement conditions. The Association also provides information to members about the FCO today. This is particularly useful at a time of radical change in the Service, when misleading rumours can abound. So, while I have perforce looked back in reflecting on my own diplomatic career, help is at hand – thanks to David Burns's initiative – if one feels the need for a clearer perception of how life is for the present generation, and of the tasks before them. And I for one certainly need assistance in hoisting in the extent of the modernisation of the information technology now used in the FCO, and the structural reforms there, as our successors address the challenges of the twenty-first century.

It is good to be back inside those walls from time to time, and to walk along the marble corridors where I so often sprinted desperately with draft telegrams and Parliamentary briefs. A number of us in my generation at the FCO feel an extra degree of rapport with the place. George Gilbert Scott's building was completed in 1868. His original, more gothic design eventually became St Pancras Station, no less; for the Foreign Office, he was asked for something more Italianate, with rich decoration to impress visitors from overseas. A century later, when post-war austerity and a phase of distaste for things Victorian had reduced the building to a sorry state of disrepair, we learned that Ministers had ruled that it was to be demolished. A ginger group among its occupants – I remember Nicholas Barrington, then in the Private Office, playing a leading part – ran a campaign to preserve it. I was a keen supporter, and was delighted when our efforts helped to generate a public outcry, and the building was reprieved.

In an about turn worthy of *Yes, Minister*, successive governments in the 1980s and 1990s refurbished the building. The decorative glories of its fine ceremonial rooms, grand staircase and main corridor were lovingly restored. In my time in FCO Departments, when one never had a moment to dwell on the images of a triumphant and bountiful Britannia around the grand staircase, it was nevertheless evident that

95. Weary parent, smart juvenile (right): Hoopoes (Upupa epops)*, Carmague 2005*

they were fading, as was the Sibyl above the door to the Secretary of State's office urging silence on those who approached. Now, when I can occasionally enjoy them at leisure, they are all in magnificent condition.

This comfortable role of supportive "Old Boy" is all that I should decently expect these days where diplomacy is concerned. My approach to birds, on the other hand, will I hope remain a bit closer to the sharp end. I have acquired my first digital camera, and am trying to get my head round that technology: I have just achieved a respectable shot of a Greenfinch (96). I shall continue to enjoy watching whatever comes along in Little Missenden and at Shardeloes and West Wycombe. Parakeets – Rose-ringed, I am sure – have caused much excitement by appearing only seven miles away. Then there will be occasional trips to places such as Minsmere, the site in Suffolk that the RSPB runs so successfully.

A spell in the Camargue each May will remain central to our French plans. An engaging spectacle down there in the spring of 2005 was the emergence of a brood of Hoopoes. As with woodpeckers, the fledgling is, on departure from the next, a smarter-looking bird than the weary parent (95). At our little house in the Var, there is no shortage of interesting birds (Crested Tits, for example – the only other place where I have seen them is the north of Scotland) and I intend to improve on my photographic efforts there.

Familiar sights will be welcome everywhere, but I aim to progress along my learning curve. I may succeed in making more sense of birds' behaviour – though some mysteries will no doubt remain. Why, for example, is the Black Woodpecker, a large and robust bird with habits similar to those of many other members of the woodpecker family, never seen in Britain, when it is common in many parts of Western Europe? Why – stranger still – are there no woodpeckers at all in Ireland, when Great Britain holds so many? I may never know.

The vision of one's Holy Grail can alter suddenly, but for the moment the principal new target for the coming season is the Kingfisher. My daughter Juliet and I are keen to get on with our joint quest to achieve really good views of this fabulous bird. A Kingfisher regularly perches by the lake where my splendid grandchildren – Oliver, Tara and Harriet – go boating; Juliet has information about their nesting pattern around

96. Digital début: Greenfinch (Chloris chloris), *Little Missenden, 2005*

97. To be emulated: Kingfisher (Alcedo atthis), *New Forest, ca 1970, by Lt Col RH Palmer*

Little Bardfield that could lead us to riches later in 2005. We shall be well satisfied if we can be half as successful as my father's shots of Kingfishers in the New Forest in the 1970s, which he took without autofocus and other modern refinements *(97)*.

Further afield, it will remain to be seen whether the lure of exotic species can overcome my growing resistance to long-distance travel. I make no promises (perhaps that should be threats).

It is as well to remain prepared for the unexpected. When I was on my sabbatical year at Harvard, I was on good terms with the staff at a local store in Cambridge, Massachusetts. The time came to say farewell to these bright and welcoming people. I told them that our next destination was our Embassy in Cuba.

"What assignment will you have there, Andy?" my friend Chris asked.

"Well, er, I'm going to be the Ambassador, actually."

Chris, rarely at a loss, was silent for several moments. Then he spoke words that were most timely for me:-

"Gee, Andy – I am really *surprised!*"

I am tempted to leave the New Englander with the last word. But I can offer a more substantial treat, in the form of an extract from *Mandarin – the Diaries of Sir Nicholas Henderson*. I have explained to Nicko that I can think of no better means of bringing to a close these musings of mine about diplomacy and birds than to quote this piece, which deals so charmingly with both themes; he has very kindly agreed to my doing so.

19 April 1976; Paris.
<u>*In a Gilded Cage.*</u>

Recently, one beautiful spring morning, a budgerigar appeared at the window of my office. It sat on the balcony rail and gave every impression of wanting to come in, of wishing to return home, which was not surprising I suppose, given the fact that my office resembles a gilded cage – even more gaudy than anything he could have escaped from. I opened the window and in it flew, perching on the ornate cornice just below the multicoloured ceiling depicting Cupid and Psyche, Bacchus and Apollo and indeed other gods in varying states of nature.

I had forgotten all about the budgerigar when my secretary announced the arrival of an official diplomatic visitor, the Ambassador of Mauritius. He was ushered into the room and I asked him to sit down on the blue satin settee. I offered him coffee and biscuits. We were chatting amicably, and even constructively, about the organisation of the Commonwealth club in Paris when the budgerigar started to show interest. It began flying in circles around His Excellency's head. The Ambassador, trained in the British tradition, remained inscrutable; and when the budgie started doing loop-the-loop just in front of his eyes he merely blinked while continuing his exposé of the kind of way he thought the Commonwealth lunches should be organised. I found it difficult to interrupt him by saying, for instance, that I was sorry but that I had just let a budgerigar in through the window. Besides, it seemed to me that he was getting used to it and it enabled him to show a truly Alec Guinness-like phlegm as the bird did a particularly tight turn round his ears. The Ambassador spoke about the importance of providing signed silver trays for all departing Ambassadors, and, as the budgie showed its appreciation by a well-timed fly-past, it occurred to me that this representative from Mauritius might regard the presence of the bird at our meeting as simply a manifestation of traditional British eccentricity. Perhaps he assumed that I always had a budgerigar flying about in my office. I decided, therefore, to continue our meeting without making any reference to it and to see whether he continued to do likewise. He did.

However as he was about to leave I turned the conversation to the flora and fauna of his native island. 'I suppose,' I said, 'you have birds like this flying about everywhere in Mauritius?'

'Well, not quite everywhere,' he replied.

The story nicely symbolises the cheering influence that birds have brought to my life, in and out of the Diplomatic Service. I am sure that, just as the words made me laugh out loud yet again as I copied them, they will bring a smile to the reader's face. I hope it is not the first to be prompted from within these covers. Either way, I send warm thanks for the companionship of all those who have come this far.

98. *On the balcony, amid the green birds of Rome: the author, with the palm that housed the breakaway Monk Parakeets, Villa Drusiana, Rome, 1993*

* Hilary Fry uses the term 'River Kingfisher' in his "Kingfishers, Bee-eaters and Rollers" (1992). *I like it! AEP*

Nightingale *(Luscinia megarhyncha)* 56
Nightjar, Greater Antillean *(Caprimulgus cubanensis)* 47
Nuthatch *(Sitta Europea)* 7

Oropendola, Montezuma *(Psarocolius montezuma)* 134 *(77)*
Osprey *(Pandion haliaetus)* 19, 149
Owl, Cuban Screech- *(Otus lawrencii)* 47 *(18, 19)*
Owl, Little *(Athene noctua)* 74, 76, 155 *(38, 39)*
Owl, Scops *(Otus scops)* 74
Owl, Stygian *(Asio stygius)* 34, 36 *(16)*
Oystercatcher *(Haematopus ostralegus)* 2, 84, 86, 151 *(42)*

Parakeet, Alexandrine *(Psittacula eupatria)* 61, 63 *(24)*
Parakeet, Monk *(Myopsitta monachus)* 58–63 *(27, 28, 31, 32)*
Parakeet, Rose-ringed *(Psittacula krameri)* 61, 163
Partridge, Grey *(Perdix perdix)* 2
Pelican, Brown *(Pelecanus occidentalis)* 17, 140
Plover, Kentish *(Chaladrius alexandrinus)* 101
Plover, Little Ringed *(Chaladrius dubius)* 101

Quetzal, Resplendent *(Pharomachrus mocinno)* 139, 144

Redshank *(Tringa totanus)* 84
Redstart *(Phoenicurus phoenicurus)* 56
Robin, American *(Turdus migratorius)* 153, 155 *(91)*
Robin, Clay-coloured *('Yigüirro') (Turdus grayi)* 147
Roller, European *(Coracias garrulus)* 123–125 *(70, 71, 72)*

Shelduck *(Tadorna tadorna)* 4
Spoonbill, Roseate *(Ajaia ajaja)* 37
Stilt, Black-winged *(Himantopus himantopus)* 113, 119 *(55, 62, 63)*
Stint, Little *(Calidris minuta)* 101
Stork, White *(Ciconia ciconia)* 107, 155 *(92)*
Swan, Mute *(Cygnus olor)* 2

Tanager, Blue and Grey *(Thraupis episcopus)* 129 *(74)*
Tanager, Scarlet-rumped *(Ramphocelus passerinii)* 136
Tanager, Stripe-headed *(Spindalis zena)* 19 *(6)*
Tern, Arctic *(Sterna paradisaea)* 17